MODERN WORLD NATIONS

AFGHANISTAN	ISRAEL
ARGENTINA	ITALY
AUSTRALIA	JAMAICA
AUSTRIA	JAPAN
BAHRAIN	KAZAKHSTAN
BANGLADESH	KENYA
BERMUDA	KUWAIT
BOLIVIA	MEXICO
BOSNIA AND HERZEGOVINA	THE NETHERLANDS
BRAZIL	NEW ZEALAND
CANADA	NIGERIA
CHILE	NORTH KOREA
CHINA	NORWAY
COLOMBIA	PAKISTAN
COSTA RICA	PERU
CROATIA	THE PHILIPPINES
CUBA	PORTUGAL
DEMOCRATIC REPUBLIC OF THE CONGO	PUERTO RICO
EGYPT	RUSSIA
ENGLAND	SAUDI ARABIA
ETHIOPIA	SCOTLAND
FRANCE	SENEGAL
REPUBLIC OF GEORGIA	SOUTH AFRICA
GERMANY	SOUTH KOREA
GHANA	SPAIN
GREECE	SWEDEN
GUATEMALA	TAIWAN
HONDURAS	THAILAND
ICELAND	TURKEY
INDIA	UKRAINE
INDONESIA	THE UNITED STATES OF AMERICA
IRAN	UZBEKISTAN
IRAQ	VENEZUELA
IRELAND	VIETNAM

England

Second Edition

Alan Allport

with additional text by George Wingfield

Series Editor
Charles F. Gritzner
South Dakota State University

CHELSEA HOUSE
PUBLISHERS

An imprint of Infobase Publishing

Frontispiece: Flag of England (the Cross of St. George)

Cover: Trafalgar Square, London.

England, Second Edition

Copyright © 2008 by Infobase Publishing

Chelsea House
An imprint of Infobase Publishing
132 West 31st Street
New York NY 10001

Library of Congress Cataloging-in-Publication Data
Allport, Alan, 1970–
England / Alan Allport ; with additional text by George Wingfield. — 2nd ed.
    p. cm. — (Modern world nations)
Includes bibliographical references and index.
ISBN-13: 978-0-7910-9514-0 (hardcover)
ISBN-10: 0-7910-9514-2 (hardcover)
1. England—Juvenile literature. [1. England.]   I. Wingfield, George.   II. Title.
III. Series.

DA27.5.A76 2007
942—dc22   2007014768

Chelsea House books are available at special discounts when purchased in bulk quantities for businesses, associations, institutions, or sales promotions. Please call our Special Sales Department in New York at (212) 967-8800 or (800) 322-8755.

You can find Chelsea House on the World Wide Web at http://www.chelseahouse.com

Series design by Takeshi Takahashi
Cover design by Joo Young An

Printed in the United States of America

Bang NMSG 10 9 8 7 6 5 4 3 2 1

This book is printed on acid-free paper.

All links and Web addresses were checked and verified to be correct at the time of publication. Because of the dynamic nature of the Web, some addresses and links may have changed since publication and may no longer be valid.

Table of Contents

1   Introducing England   8

2   Physical Landscapes   14

3   England Through Time   27

4   People and Culture   43

5   Government and Politics   61

6   England's Economy   75

7   Living in England Today   89

8   England's Heritage and Treasures   103

9   England Looks Ahead   110

    Facts at a Glance   114
    History at a Glance   117
    Bibliography   120
    Further Reading   121
    Index   122

England

Second Edition

1

Introducing England

In William Shakespeare's play *The Life and Death of King Richard II* the king's dying uncle and councilman, John of Gaunt, delivers a fiery patriotic speech that has become one of the classic statements of English national pride:

> This royal throne of kings, this sceptered isle . . .
> This fortress built by Nature for herself
> Against infection and the hand of war,
> This happy breed of men, this little world,
> This precious stone set in the silver sea,
> Which serves it in the office of a wall,
> Or as a moat defensive to a house,
> Against the envy of less happier lands,
> This blessed plot, this earth, this realm, this England.

These are inspiring words, as centuries of Englishmen have attested; but John of Gaunt's passionate speech includes one puzzling but rarely mentioned mistake—England is not an island! Shakespeare did make occasional geographical blunders in his plays, partly out of ignorance—he once suggested that Bohemia in the modern-day Czech Republic has deserts and coastlines, when it has neither—but it is safe to assume that the Bard of Avon was familiar with his own country's physical features. Should we assume that this was an extreme piece of poetic license?

What Shakespeare was perhaps doing, through the words of John of Gaunt, was confusing *England*—a single kingdom bordering Scotland and Wales—with *Great Britain*, an island containing all three countries. We should probably not be too hard on the playwright. For hundreds of years people inside and outside of England have been making this same basic error of definition. The details of English life do not help matters much. People speak of the queen of England—but also the British government; the British Army—but equally the Church of England; and the English language—spoken within the former British Empire. The British fly the Union Jack, but this is not the national flag of England, which is the Cross of St. George (a red cross on a white background, which also forms part of the Union Jack). To confuse things further, the Republic of Ireland is within the British Isles but is definitely not part of Great Britain—as any Irish citizen will gladly inform you. And good luck to anyone traveling to Glasgow or Cardiff who dares to call the locals "English"!

Any book introducing England, then, should begin with an explanation of its terminology. The *British Isles* is a geographical, not a political, unit. It is the collective name for the islands in the northwest corner of Europe, bounded on one side by the Atlantic Ocean and on the other by the North Sea. There are two principal islands, Great Britain and Ireland, and a host of

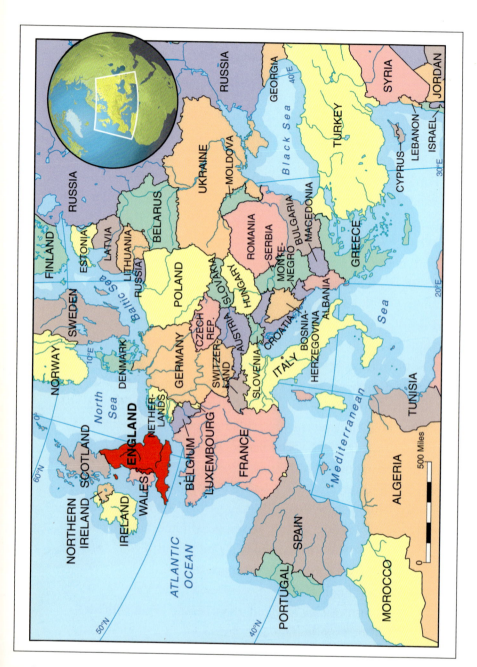

England is located off the northwestern European mainland and shares borders with Scotland (to the north) and Wales (to the west). The country is approximately 50,000 square miles (130,000 square kilometers), or about the size of Alabama.

much smaller ones such as the Isle of Man, the Isle of Wight, the Scottish Hebrides, and the tiny archipelagos of the Orkneys and the Shetlands. *Great Britain* is the largest of the British Isles and it contains three countries—England, Scotland, and Wales—each of which was once independent but now are combined in a single state. In common terminology, Great Britain is often shortened to just *Britain*. The people of Great Britain are usually called collectively the *British* or, if referring to individuals, *Britons*. Along with *Northern Ireland*, sometimes known as *Ulster* or the *Six Counties*, these countries make up the *United Kingdom*, or *U.K.* for short. To think of a North American analogy, England is to the United Kingdom what South Dakota or California is to the United States.

This analogy is not quite correct, however, because England is by far the largest, most populous, and richest of the four members of the United Kingdom. Historically, this has meant that England has tended to dominate the British Isles, sometimes by diplomatic and economic means and sometimes by bloodier military methods. England's relationship with its neighbors has not always been a happy one. Echoes of disharmony have until recently been apparent, for example, in the religious and ethnic conflict in Northern Ireland. However, it is a relationship that is open to continuous change, and one of the political developments of recent years has been an increase in the local autonomy of the non-English regions of the United Kingdom. For example, the new Scottish parliament now sits in Edinburgh and, in 2007, a power-sharing government including both Unionists and Irish Republicans was agreed and formed in Northern Ireland. The increasing decentralization of the United Kingdom creates questions about England's identity and future, something to which we will return.

The proliferation of English words, place-names, and associations across the world from New Zealand to Alaska indicates the profound influence that this relatively small country has had in international affairs. Both the United States and Canada

London is England's capital and largest city, with a population of approximately 7.5 million. Both Tower Bridge, which crosses the River Thames (foreground), and St. Paul's Cathedral (background), which has the second-largest dome in the world, are pictured in this aerial view of the city.

were originally founded as English colonies, and millions of modern-day Americans can trace their ancestry back to English emigrants who left the mother country for a new life sometime during the last four centuries. England has an unusually long tradition of unbroken social institutions, such as its Royal Family and Parliament. The country's rich legacy of monarchs, castles, and pomp and circumstance makes it one of the world's most popular tourist destinations. History aside, England is also a major economic center and its capital, London, is one of the hubs of the global financial marketplace. The huge city also continues to wield important political and diplomatic power. At the beginning of the twentieth century, England was at the heart of the largest empire in the history of the world. Although that empire has since fragmented, England will have an important role to play in the affairs of the twenty-first century, although precisely what that role will be is not so clear.

Shakespeare's suggestion that the sea served England "in the office of a wall or as a moat defensive to a house" now seems long outdated. A direct rail link through the Channel Tunnel (the "Chunnel") from France and the rest of Europe and innumerable flights and ferries that operate unceasingly bring people from every corner of the globe to England. Large-scale immigration over the last 50 years has brought huge numbers of foreigners to England, many of whom have become naturalized as British citizens. Initially they came from what was formerly the British Empire, but is now called the Commonwealth. Since the United Kingdom joined the European Union, many immigrants have come from other countries in Europe. This upsurge in immigration over the past two decades, both legal and illegal, has seen an influx from countries with no particular ties to Britain. This immigration has caused both benefits and problems. It has resulted in a population very different from that of England a hundred years ago, one that is increasingly multicultural. It is effectively a nonmilitary invasion that Shakespeare could never have envisaged.

Physical Landscapes

E ngland is only a part of the United Kingdom, but it is geographically the major part, taking up about 50,000 (130,000 square kilometers) of the United Kingdom's roughly 94,000 square miles (244,000 square kilometers) in area. This means that England is approximately the size of Alabama. England forms the southern, and largest, portion of the island of Great Britain, with Wales to its west and Scotland to its north. Although Great Britain is often thought of as being a very small place, it is actually the eighth-largest island in the world, stretching some 600 miles (966 kilometers) from its northern to its southern extremities.

The British Isles lie at the northwestern corner of the European mainland, surrounded by several bodies of water. To the south and southeast is the English Channel, which divides England from France. At its narrowest point, between Dover and Calais, the two countries are a mere 21 miles (34 kilometers) apart. It is here that the Channel

Much of southern England is flat, consisting of lush farmland, which is watered by a number of rivers, including the Thames. Conversely, the northern part of the country, near the Scottish border, is composed of hilly moorlands and deep freshwater lakes.

Tunnel was built from 1987–1994, creating a rail-link under the seabed between England and Europe.

Eastern Britain is separated from Scandinavia, the Low Countries, and Germany by the North Sea, a shallow and stormy arm of the Atlantic Ocean. One area of the North Sea, the rich fishing zone known as the Dogger Bank, is barely 50 feet (15 meters) deep in places. Western Ireland and the north and southwest coasts of Great Britain lie directly on the Atlantic Ocean shoreline. Ireland and Britain themselves are divided by the Irish Sea, which lets out into the Atlantic via two conduits, the narrow North Channel Strait and the broader St. George's Channel to the south.

All these seas and waterways have had an important influence on the development of English history. Although England has no great river systems, its coast is pockmarked with dozens of bays and inlets that make excellent natural harbors. The convoluted path of the coastline means that no part of the country is more than 75 miles (121 kilometers) from tidal water. And Great Britain's position astride the shipping lanes of northern Europe gives it an important strategic significance. The wisdom of possessing a strong navy has been something that monarchs and governments in England have been very conscious of for more than 500 years. All of these factors have encouraged Englishmen throughout the ages to look to the seas for their economic and military strength.

LAND FEATURES

England's coastline was one of the last to stabilize in Europe, parts of it only reaching their present-day form around 5000 B.C. Not that long before then, the island of Great Britain was still physically connected to the European mainland. A land corridor existed across what would become the English Channel, and much of what is now the North Sea was above sea level. These very recent changes—"recent" in the geological sense—have helped give England a complex and multilayered mineral structure. Broadly speaking, the farther west and north one goes, the older the rock becomes. Ancient, dense igneous (volcanic) formations on the upland plateaus of Cornwall and Cumbria complement much newer alluvial deposits in the flat East Anglian basin. Sandstone, limestone, slate, and chalk banks crisscross the country, sometimes folded into small hill chains. Rich coal seams in Kent, Nottingham, Yorkshire, and Tyneside have proven vitally important to England's industrial and economic development. They were formed from plant remains that built up in prehistoric times when much of the country was a moist, humid swamp. England's fossil, rock, and soil record is so intriguing that it is hardly surprising to discover that the modern science of geology was founded by an Englishman, William Smith, who published his national geological survey in 1815—the first such systematic study in the world.

CLIMATE

England is located between about 50 and 56°N, on the same latitude as most of Ontario and Quebec. It lies mostly between longitude 3°W and 1°E. The Greenwich Meridian, 0° longitude, which divides the world into the Eastern and Western hemispheres, is measured from the old Royal Observatory in the London suburb of Greenwich. In normal circumstances, England's high latitude position would have given the country a rather forbidding climate, with bitter winters and lots of snow. However, the British Isles are blessed by a weather phenomenon known as the Gulf Stream. Warm water from the tropical Caribbean Sea and Gulf of Mexico is channeled along the North American coastline before it swings eastward across the Atlantic to form the North Atlantic Current. This makes the local sea temperature around Great Britain and Ireland considerably higher than it would otherwise register. One of the biggest long-term concerns the British have about changes in global weather patterns, possibly caused by environmental damage, is that the

Gulf Stream may one day cease to flow. Were this to happen, it would cause a sharp and disastrous drop in temperatures around the British Isles.

Because of the Gulf Stream, England has a temperate climate, neither unduly hot in summer nor cold in winter. Temperatures typically reach about 70 to 80°F (22 to 27°C) in July and August, then dip to just above freezing (0°C) in January. There is generally some snow in the winter months, but rarely of blizzard proportions. Other than flooding and coastal erosion, which as we will see below is a serious ecological dilemma, England has no other weather extremes. It does not experience tornadoes, hurricanes, or severe heat waves.

It is rather ironic that this mild and unassuming climate should have gotten such a terrible reputation! The Roman writer Tacitus was the first foreigner to describe England's weather as "objectionable," and ever since then it has become a standing joke that the country has the worst weather in the world. The problem is that the same Gulf Stream currents that bring such vital warm water also are the source of moisture-drenched cloud banks. These clouds, which have picked up plenty of Atlantic Ocean moisture along the way, break across the western British Isles and regularly douse much of Britain and Ireland in rain showers. More than 65 inches (165 centimeters) of rain will fall annually on average in the wettest English region—the northwestern Lake District. England's green and pleasant landscape owes its existence to regular precipitation. But that is small comfort to the local population who must endure what can seem like endless, dreary rainy days. Clouds also obscure much of the natural sunlight, making England a frequently gray, overcast country. Fickleness of the weather has turned into a major preoccupation of conversation for many in England. The nation's television viewers often sit glumly as they listen to the usual unpromising updates from the meteorological office every day.

The rolling farmland and woodlands of Oxfordshire, just to the west of London, are indicative of southern England's landscape, where the majority of the country's agricultural production takes place. Pictured here is a bucolic scene near the village of Swinbrook, Oxfordshire.

ENGLAND'S GEOGRAPHICAL ZONES
Southern England

For convenience, England can be divided into four zones on the basis of its physical geography. The first is Southern England, from Land's End at the westernmost part of the Cornwall Peninsula, to the port of Dover in Kent. Traditionally, the lush

Located on the English Channel, the Seven Sisters chalk cliffs form part of the South Downs in southeastern England's East Sussex County. The cliffs are often used as a stand-in for movies that feature the White Cliffs of Dover, which are no longer white.

lowlands of this region have provided the best of Great Britain's farming zones, and before the onset of northern industrialization in the nineteenth century, most population growth was concentrated here—as it is once again with the recent decline in heavy industry. The River Thames flows eastward 215 miles (346 kilometers) from its source in Gloucestershire's Cotswold Hills to its sea outlet in the Thames estuary. The southeastern valley of the Thames has long been an area of human settlement, with the sprawling metropolis of Greater London at its hub; the Thames flows right through the center of the city. Immediately surrounding London are the so-called "Home Counties," which include Buckinghamshire, Hertfordshire, Kent, Essex, and Surrey. Major parts of these once distinct regions have become steadily swallowed up by the capital's growth, but are popular with London workers who commute from their homes by train every day. Farther south are the Channel ports, such as Portsmouth, Southampton, Folkestone, and Dover. Brighton, also on the coast, has been a popular resort and vacation destination for centuries. Southeastern England is mostly flat, but there are two modest parallel uplands running east/west, known as the North Downs and the South Downs.

Southwestern England is much more rugged and forbidding. The "West Country," as it is known, remained a comparatively lawless area until the early eighteenth century. Its coastline, particularly that of Cornwall, was the haunt of smugglers and "wreckers" who attempted to lure passing ships onto the rocks at night with false signals in order to seize their cargoes.

Cornwall also has many ancient sacred sites with prehistoric standing stones, stone circles, and similar monuments. These mostly date from Neolithic times (4000–2000 B.C. in Britain), and our knowledge of the people who constructed them and the purpose for which they were built is sparse. Cornwall and Somerset, too, are counties where many ancient legends took root both before and after the Roman Invasion of Britain in 55 B.C. (which we shall come to later). It is this part of the West Country that is chiefly associated with the tales of King Arthur and his Knights of the Round Table and, indeed, the Quest for the Holy Grail.

Dartmoor and Exmoor are the region's two characteristic national parks, wild expanses of moorland with a desolate beauty. Farther north and east is the county of Gloucestershire, which straddles the Severn estuary, and south of it on the

River Avon, is the port of Bristol. This has been an important trading and maritime center since the Middle Ages, and it was the starting point for John Cabot's first expedition to North America in 1497. The Avon, which connects Bristol to the sea via its tidal lower reaches, flows out into the Severn estuary that forms part of the larger Bristol Channel. This is an arm of the Atlantic Ocean dividing England's West Country from Wales, through which all shipping to Bristol and South Wales must pass.

The Midlands and East Anglia

Central England is made up of the East and West Midlands and the flat but fertile fenlands of East Anglia. The Midlands are Shakespeare country, focused particularly on the immortal Bard's birthplace of Stratford-upon-Avon, which is also the modern-day home of the Royal Shakespeare Theater Company. (Note that this River Avon is different than the one that flows through Bath and Bristol.) We shall return to Shakespeare later on.

The Midlands are also heavily industrialized, containing England's second-largest city, Birmingham, and some equally built-up metropolitan areas such as Wolverhampton, Coventry, and Nottingham. Much of the West Midlands region is known as the "Black Country" because of the thick coatings of grime and coal dust that became familiar to its residents during the Industrial Revolution. Although the Midlands acquired a lot of their wealth from the production of heavy manufacturing goods and the automobile industry, the region is also famous for fine pottery and ceramics.

The marshy fenlands in north Cambridgeshire and west Norfolk cut off that region from the rest of England for centuries, and even now its population density is unusually low. These fenlands have now been mostly drained, but the region continues to resemble the flat polder country of the Netherlands more than it does other parts of the United Kingdom. The market town of Norwich and the great university city of Cambridge are among the more important urban centers. East

Anglia's farmland has especially rich soil and provides much of Britain's cereal, potato crop, and other root vegetable needs.

Yorkshire and the Northwest

As we progress farther northward, the country begins to be divided by a great hill chain called the Pennines—sometimes called the "backbone of England"—which begins in the Peak District and continues northward toward the Scottish border. Lying roughly on either side of the Pennines are the historic rival counties of Lancashire in the west and Yorkshire in the east. Lancashire traditionally boasted two enormous industrial regions, the great manufacturing hub of Manchester and the Atlantic port of Liverpool. But each of these cities has now been given a special administrative status of its own. Yorkshire, too, has several important industrial cities, such as Leeds, Hull, and Sheffield. All of these nineteenth-century behemoths have suffered enormously due to the decline of heavy industry in the last hundred years, and the Pennine counties—perhaps England's nearest equivalent to the U.S. "rust belt"—have suffered relative depopulation. However, economic woes have not dispelled any of Yorkshire's or Lancashire's local civic pride, which includes use of incomprehensible regional accents and a "straight-talking" attitude toward life that is contrasted unfavorably with that of the supposedly more effete south. This region is one of the best examples of the stark contrast between England's rural beauty and its grittier industrial legacy. Handsome river valleys and moorlands provide a contrast with disused factory chimneys and the now closed or demolished textile mills. The West Yorkshire Moors, famous for their association with the novels of the Brontë sisters, Emily and Charlotte, are right next door to the former cotton metropolis of Bradford.

Northern England

Everyone in England recognizes a difference in character between the north and the south of the country, but there is much dispute about where the boundary between the two lies;

Despite its wet and windy weather, the Lake District of northwestern England is a popular tourist destination for the English. Pictured here is the Lake District National Park in the county of Cumbria, which is one of 14 national parks in the United Kingdom.

no "Mason-Dixon line" exists to clarify the issue. An old joke says that the north begins outside of Watford, just a few miles from Greater London! A more realistic line of division would be from the Mersey to the Humber river estuaries, on the southern fringes of Lancashire and Yorkshire. For our current purposes, however, northern England will be taken to mean the region nearest to Scotland, especially the large counties of Northumberland, Durham, and Cumbria. This is historically disputed land, which throughout the centuries often changed hands with the Scots and was the scene of bitter battles and sieges. Its military importance is reflected in the large number of surviving medieval castles, such as Alnwick, and the great Roman fortification of Hadrian's Wall.

Cumbria is home to the Lake District, a region of hilly moorlands and deep freshwater lakes that is arguably England's most picturesque region and best-known "beauty spot." The Lake District contains England's highest point, Scafell Pike, which is only 3,210 feet (978 meters) above sea level and is easily manageable by hill-walkers. It also boasts the country's principal body of freshwater, 10.5-mile-long (16.9-kilometer-long) Lake Windermere. While less spectacular, Northumberland also contains some ruggedly attractive scenery such as the Cheviot Hills. The Tyne and Tees river estuaries form a large industrial area that includes Newcastle and Middlesbrough, once major shipbuilding and iron-working centers, but now fallen on harder times.

ENVIRONMENTAL CONCERNS

Because of the rapid pace of their country's industrialization, the English were among the first people in the world to become seriously concerned about the effects of pollution on their natural environment. This is not to say that the problem of pollution was tackled quickly. As late as the 1950s, cities such as London were grimy and blackened, with terrible public health records. The famous London fogs in the late Victorian era were actually formed by belching chimney smoke. These thick smoky "pea-soupers" of Sherlock Holmes legend were responsible for the premature deaths of thousands of people from respiratory-related illnesses. Even 50 years later, London was often plagued by dense smog, much of which came from coal-burning electric power stations that had been built alongside the River Thames during the 1930s. But the pioneering 1956 Clean Air Act forced industrial manufacturers to implement more effective pollution controls. This legislation made England's towns and cities much more pleasant places in which to work and reside.

Certainly the replacement of household fireplaces with gas and electric heating helped to sweeten the urban air. Ironically, the collapse of England's industrial base also shut off its factory smokestacks and thus contributed to an overall improvement in air quality. Industrial decline also helped reduce the number of pollutants in the water supply. England at the turn of the twenty-first century is a much healthier place to live than it was a century ago. Nonetheless, there are still major international controversies over acid rain produced by the country's coal-burning power stations and slight contamination of seawater by radioactive waste from nuclear reactors.

If the more pessimistic projections about rising world sea levels caused by the "greenhouse effect" are accurate, then England's greatest ecological threat in the new century may come from persistent flooding of low-lying land. Because no part of England is more than 75 miles (121 kilometers) from tidal waters, few areas are completely safe from the effects of higher sea levels. Already the winter inundation of several areas of England close to major rivers has become a dreaded almost-annual event. And the government is under increasing pressure to construct sophisticated defenses such as London's Thames Barrier (a tidal barrage inaugurated in 1984) in other vulnerable regions. The erosion of spectacular shoreline cliffs has combined with this problem; as the softer rocks of the coast are steadily worn away, the flat and unprotected land behind them becomes open to the sea and may even be permanently covered by saltwater. England's coastal outline, which was thought to have stabilized some 7,000 years ago, may be on the move again. It is partly for this reason that "Green" issues have come to the forefront of many British people's concerns. As a result, important environmental pressure groups such as Greenpeace and Friends of the Earth have gained in prominence.

3

England Through Time

England, its people boast, has not been successfully invaded by a foreign country since 1066. This is a bit misleading, because some English kings were overthrown by "pretenders" to the throne with the support of foreign powers and the threat of their armies abroad. Both Edward II (1284–1327) and James II (1633–1701) were removed from power in this way, for example. But it is true that England is one of the oldest continually existing states in the world, with an unbroken line of succession dating back more than a thousand years. From the Spanish Armada in 1588 to Napoleon Bonaparte's fleet in 1805, to Nazi Germany's Air Force in 1940, the English have beaten back successive waves of would-be invaders from mainland Europe. This has to some extent encouraged the English to think of themselves as a people apart. They live aloof from the rest of the continent in "splendid isolation," developing their own unique customs and traditions.

No country is truly isolated, however, and in fact England has been in continuous interaction with the rest of the British Isles, mainland Europe, and the world since its earliest times. Modern England owes its language, its religions, its legal and political institutions, and the diversity of its population to influences from abroad. No country that has had so many foreign empires—in medieval France, in Ireland, in North America, and eventually in Africa, Asia, and India—could expect to be unchanged as a result.

PREHISTORIC ENGLAND

As mentioned in Chapter 2, up to about 8,000 years ago Great Britain was still physically connected to the rest of Europe by a land bridge. This allowed wandering tribes of hunters and gatherers to cross from France into southern England, and over the centuries they slowly expanded across the rest of the then British peninsula. No one knows for sure when the first humans arrived in Britain, but the oldest remains ever discovered are 500,000 years old and date from the Paleolithic (Old Stone Age) period. During the last ice age, which came to an end around 10,000 years ago, much of northern Britain was covered by glaciers and forbidding Arctic tundra. The gradual retreat of the ice brought a warming of the land and coastal waters, encouraging thick forests rich in wildlife to emerge. Rising sea levels also swallowed up the land bridge. The higher temperatures made England more habitable, but also cut it off from developments in the rest of Europe. For this reason, new technologies such as farming (from 4000 B.C.), the use of bronze (2000–700 B.C.), and the making of iron implements (500–0 B.C.) were relatively slow to arrive in England.

The first identifiable English civilization is known as "Windmill Hill," named for the archeological site near Avebury in Wiltshire, where its remains were discovered. Windmill Hill society, which developed around 6,000 years ago, was based on agriculture and animal husbandry. Its people used flint tools

Designated a UNESCO (United Nations Educational, Scientific, and Cultural Organization) World Heritage Site in 1986, Stonehenge is one of England's most famous landmarks. The Bronze Age monument, which is located in the county of Wiltshire in southwestern England, is composed of a henge earthwork containing a circle of large standing stones.

and had complex religious rites and burial customs. About 2000 B.C., Windmill Hill culture was supplanted by the so-called "Beaker" people who emigrated from what is now the Netherlands and northern Germany. These people were named after the distinctively shaped pottery beakers that archeologists often found in their burial sites. In addition to more advanced metal-working skills and trading patterns—Beaker goods have been found as far away as the eastern Mediterranean—they constructed elaborate monuments and stone circles. By far the most famous of their works is Stonehenge on Salisbury Plain, also in Wiltshire. Stonehenge had apparently long been an important ritual site, but the Beaker people erected the massive stone slabs that we see there today. Some of these mighty monoliths weigh 50 tons and were shaped from sarsen stones found on the Marlborough Downs 20 miles (32 kilometers) away. Other smaller "bluestones" were specially brought from Wales, more than 200 miles (322 kilometers) away. No one is really sure what the purpose of Stonehenge was. Because of its particular alignment to the extreme positions of the rising and setting of the sun and moon, it has been suggested that it may have been used as a sort of astronomical calendar to indicate the changing seasons.

Between 700 and 300 B.C., small groups of migrants from mainland Europe brought Celtic culture to England. The Celts had knowledge of iron working, and made beautifully decorated weapons and armor. They exploited the tin mines of Cornwall for the first time, trading tin for Italian silver that their chieftains jealously guarded in newly constructed hill forts. For all their artisan skills and achievements, however, the Celts would prove no match for invaders from the south who were to bring significant change to England.

ROMAN ENGLAND

In 55 B.C., the Roman general and statesman Julius Caesar, who was campaigning in Gaul (modern-day France), made a tentative raid on Kent. He and his troops soon left for other adventures, but the Romans did not forget about this dark corner of the known world, which they referred to as "Britannia." Almost a hundred years later, one of Caesar's successors, Emperor Claudius, decided to return—and this time, for good. In A.D. 43, he sent four legions of elite Roman infantry across the Channel, and in a lightning campaign subdued all of the native Celtic tribes of southeastern England. During the next 40 years, the Romans conquered the rest of England and Wales and established a frontier along the modern border with Scotland. For the next 400 years, England would be part of the classical Roman civilization from the Mediterranean region.

Roman dominance did not go unchallenged. In A.D. 60, a Celtic queen, Boudicca, from what is now East Anglia, led a rebellion against the cruel policies of the Roman governor. Her tribal warriors sacked several forts and towns (including London, then a small settlement) until they were defeated at the hands of the legions. Boudicca committed suicide, but her proud stand against tyranny later became a symbol of English nationhood. One of the stranger details of her story is that, according to legend, the site of her burial was under what is now Platform 10 of King's Cross railroad station in London. The Romans also suffered persistent raiding from the native tribes in Scotland. Rather than conquer such a thinly populated country, Emperor Hadrian ordered the construction of a huge defensive wall across Britannia's northern border, from the Solway Firth to Tyneside. Hadrian's Wall, much of which stands to this day, is a triumph of Roman engineering.

During the centuries of Roman occupation, settlers moved from elsewhere in the empire and built sophisticated towns, roads, and fortifications. Spectacular examples of Roman building and artistry can still be seen in places such as the spa-town of Bath, where the colonists used the local hot mineral springs to construct an elaborate bathhouse combined with a temple that is dedicated to the goddess Minerva. Many modern English cities such as London, Manchester, York, Canterbury, and Carlisle were founded as Roman military or civilian settlements.

The Celtic people who had been pushed back by the Romans to Cornwall, Wales, and Ireland were credited with the founding of some of the early Christian churches in the West. According to legend, the earliest church in Britain was founded at Glastonbury in southwestern England in the latter part of the first century A.D. It was not until A.D. 597, however, that papal missionaries from Rome first arrived in England—long after Roman rule had been abandoned.

THE DARK AGES

In A.D. 410, the Emperor Honorius, beleaguered by barbarian invasions elsewhere, sent a proclamation to the Romans in Britannia informing them that the imperial army could no longer defend them. They would henceforth have to look after themselves. With this abdication of responsibility, the Roman presence in England effectively ended. Not that there was still a distinctive "Roman" community there anyway. By the fifth century A.D., many of the colonists had intermarried with the local Celtic peoples and consequently had become largely indistinguishable from the natives. But the departure of the Roman legions left England dangerously unprotected against foreign invaders.

The period between the fifth and eleventh centuries is sometimes called the "Dark Ages" because so little written evidence remains from it. We know that England was attacked in the 400s by successive waves of pagan tribes from northwestern Europe—Frisians, Jutes, Angles, and Saxons. These invaders, collectively known as the "Anglo-Saxons," drove much of the original Romano-British population out of England, causing them to retreat to Cornwall, Wales, and even as far as Brittany on the French coast. After they had exhausted their appetite for looting and pillaging, the Anglo-Saxons began to settle England permanently. The country lost its political unity and was subdivided into many rival kingdoms. Among the most important were Wessex (land of the West Saxons) in the southwest, Mercia in the Midlands, and Northumbria in the north. During the seventh century A.D., the Anglo-Saxons were mainly converted to Christianity by missionaries from Ireland and others sent from Rome, such as St. Augustine of Canterbury.

In the ninth and tenth centuries, a new breed of barbarian invaders appeared; these were the Vikings, or Norsemen, of Scandinavia. For decades the Viking raiders caused terror and destruction throughout England, but eventually, like the Anglo-Saxons before them, they chose to establish a permanent presence. This was short-lived, however, because the Kingdom of Wessex was on the rise. Between 926 and 937, one of its rulers, Athelstan, retook the Viking territories in the north of England and became the first Anglo-Saxon monarch of a reunited England. After Athelstan's reign, England was never again a politically divided country.

THE NORMAN CONQUEST AND THE MIDDLE AGES

In 1066, one of Athelstan's descendants, St. Edward the Confessor, an exceptionally pious king who built the original Westminster Abbey, died without an heir. The earl of Wessex, Harold, claimed the English throne. Edward's French cousin, William of Normandy, also sought this rich prize, claiming that Edward had promised it to him, and so he promptly invaded England. Their armies met at Hastings in Sussex on October 14, 1066, and after a fierce battle, Harold was killed. The victor, now known as William the Conqueror, marched in triumph to London and so began the Norman kingship of England.

William and the Anglo-French kings who followed him left a powerful impression on English history. The Norman aristocracy imposed the "feudal" system throughout England, in which society was divided into social classes—peasantry, knights, and barons, with the king at the top. Each paid homage to their superiors by service or payment. William ordered the construction of castles throughout his kingdom and made a tax survey of the whole country that was compiled as the *Domesday Book*. Much of the shire county system of regional English government dates from the Norman period.

The Norman kings of England were eventually replaced by another related dynasty, the Plantagenets. Thanks to their Norman inheritance, the Plantagenet monarchs remained powerful landholders in France, and throughout the Middle Ages many kings and queens of England spent more time in France than they did in their "homeland" (and spoke better French than English, too). Edward III even claimed the French throne for himself, and so set off the "Hundred Years' War" between the two countries. Despite impressive English victories at battles such as Crecy (1346) and Agincourt (1415), the French eventually rallied and fought off the Plantagenet threat.

One reason that the English failed to hold on to their gains was that this was the time of the "Black Death"—an epidemic of bubonic plague—that decimated the English population, eventually killing about one-third of the people. By the mid-1400s, most of the English possessions in France had been lost, and England's kings were in any case preoccupied with domestic conflict back across the Channel.

THE WAR OF THE ROSES AND THE REFORMATION

Edward III's successors were divided between the dynasties, or "houses," of York and Lancaster. The struggle between the two houses, which came to dominate the fifteenth century, was known as the War of the Roses because of the Yorkist and Lancastrian symbols—a white rose and a red rose, respectively. The war seemed to end in 1483 with the coronation of Richard III, a powerful Yorkist king. But rumors that Richard had murdered his two young nephews, the "Princes in the Tower," one of whom was his deposed predecessor, King Edward V, destabilized his regime and he was killed two years later at the Battle of Bosworth Field by Henry VII of the Welsh Tudor dynasty.

Henry VII's reign brought much-needed stability to the country, but his son and successor, Henry VIII, created new strife, this time religious. Henry's marriage to Catherine of Aragon had produced no male heir, and so he wished to divorce her and marry a younger woman, Anne Boleyn. This required the permission of the pope, who was at the time busy trying to suppress Martin Luther's Protestant heresy in Germany and so dared not alienate Catherine's nephew, the Holy Roman Emperor Charles V. Henry grew exasperated by papal stalling, and finally in 1533 ordered Parliament to pass an "Act of Supremacy" making him, the king, the head of the new Church

During his reign, King Henry VII expanded Windsor Castle, transforming it from a palace to a fortress. One of his most important additions was the castle's main entrance gate (pictured here), which served as an effective barrier to any outside threat.

of England, which would henceforth be totally independent of Catholic Rome. Almost by accident, England had become a Protestant country.

Henry went through six wives in the end, and the children of his various marriages had very different ideas about the new Church. Henry's son, Edward VI, was a staunch Protestant, but reigned too briefly to have much influence. Edward's sister, Mary I, was an equally rigid Catholic; during her five years on the throne, she persecuted English Protestants and became known as "Bloody Mary" for executing hundreds of religious dissenters. The sister who succeeded her, Elizabeth I, was a compromiser. Although she kept England independent of Rome and angered extremists of both sides, Elizabeth sought—and achieved—an important measure of religious stability.

THE BIRTH OF BRITAIN

Few people would have guessed at her coronation that the young and inexperienced Elizabeth would become "Good Queen Bess," the ruler of England for more than 40 years and one of the nation's greatest monarchs. Her finest hour was in 1588, when Philip II of Spain, Mary I's widower, who was fanatically determined to return England to Catholicism, launched a huge fleet in an attempt to invade England and reassert papal authority. Philip's "Spanish Armada" was defeated by Elizabeth's warships (with the help of bad weather) and the victory signaled England's beginnings as a great naval power.

Elizabeth died childless and unmarried, known as the "Virgin Queen." Her successor as king of England was James I of the House of Stuart, who already ruled Scotland as James VI. This royal union between the two countries, which had traditionally been at loggerheads, was a watershed in the history of the British Isles. Wales had already united with England in 1283, and now James, who called himself the first "King of Great Britain," was the undisputed ruler of the whole island. Unification, however, was far from complete. England and Scotland still maintained separate parliaments until 1707, when the Act of Union formally merged the two countries into a single state—the United Kingdom—administered from London. A similar Act of Union with Ireland would follow in 1801. In theory at least, there were no more English, Scottish, Welsh, or Irish people—there were only "Britons."

CIVIL WARS AND REVOLUTIONS

Before this national unification was complete, however, the English had to undergo three traumatic revolutions against the authority of their kings. James's son Charles I was an autocratic monarch who sought to rule England without the assistance of Parliament. This provoked so much hostility that fighting broke out between factions of the country loyal to the Crown (the "Cavaliers") and those who supported the liberties of Parliament (the "Roundheads"). The civil war of the 1640s ended with Charles under arrest; he was publicly executed at Westminster as a traitor in 1649. This stunning decision was followed by the creation of the 11-year Protectorate under the parliamentarian general Oliver Cromwell. In reality the protectorate was really a republic, the only such government in English history.

By the time of Cromwell's death in 1658, the protectorate had become extremely unpopular, and the English people welcomed the return of the dead king's son, Charles II, to the throne. But Charles showed signs of sympathy for Catholicism, and his brother James II, who was his successor, was an openly avowed Catholic. This was too much for the Protestant parliament, and it secretly invited James's son-in-law, the Dutchman William of Orange, to seize power in a military coup. William landed in England in 1688, and in the so-called Glorious Revolution deposed James, who fled to France. William was confirmed as the new monarch, although on the firm understanding that henceforth Parliament would make most day-to-day political decisions.

The American War of Independence can also be seen as the third in this series of insurrections against English royal authority. England's first colony in North America was founded at Jamestown in Virginia in 1607 during James I's reign. During the century that followed, a string of English settlements were established on the eastern seaboard, from Georgia to Newfoundland. France's defeat in the French and Indian War of 1756–1763 guaranteed the colonists' safety from foreign invasion, but it also made them less tolerant of London's sometimes high-handed governance. In 1775, the colonists, following the tradition established by the British parliament in the 1640s and 1680s, revolted against their "tyrant" king, George III. The war, never popular in Britain, ended with the formation of the United States of America and the creation of a second English-speaking Atlantic power.

Of far greater concern to England than the loss of the American colonies were events that took place soon afterwards in France. In 1789, the French Revolution swept the monarchy of Louis XVI and his queen, Marie Antoinette, from power, and three years later a republic was declared. The king and queen were tried for treason and subsequently they and many other French aristocrats were guillotined in Paris. England and the other monarchies of Europe shuddered. New military alliances were sought out and agreed to combat this rising tide of republicanism. It was during the turmoil of these times in revolutionary France that Napoleon Bonaparte rose to power becoming first consul in 1799 and crowning himself emperor in 1804. For the next 10 years, the French under Napoleon conquered much of Europe during the Napoleonic Wars. At times it seemed that England stood alone against Napoleon, and a French invasion was feared. But the decisive naval battle of Trafalgar (1805) and later the defeat of Napoleon's army at Waterloo in what is now Belgium (1815) by the combined armies of the British, Germans, Belgians, Dutch, and Prussians—although French troops outnumbered them—finally brought this dangerous threat to

In 1805, the Royal (British) Navy defeated a combined French and Spanish fleet at the Battle of Trafalgar. The decisive victory, in which the French and Spanish lost 22 ships and the British nary a one, solidified Great Britain's reputation as the world's foremost naval power.

an end. Napoleon was sent into permanent exile, and the French monarchy was restored under King Louis XVIII.

THE INDUSTRIAL REVOLUTION

While political revolt was taking place in America in the late 1700s, a less bloody but just as important economic upheaval was happening in England at the same time—the phenomenon known as the Industrial Revolution. This was the introduction of new factory methods and energy sources such as wind, water, coal, and steam to create a massive increase in economic production. Starting with textiles and moving on to iron and eventually steelmaking, England became by the early nineteenth century the industrial powerhouse of the world. The effects of these new technologies were immense. Enormous cities, such as Manchester, Liverpool, Leeds, and Sheffield, dominated by smoke-belching factories, grew up within a single generation. Steam-powered railroads, invented in England, connected all parts of the country for the first time.

Middle-class businessmen grew rich on factory profits and demanded representation in Parliament. Working-class trade unionists also insisted on more political power, as well as social legislation to restrict poor working conditions and improve appalling slum housing. The Industrial Revolution changed the shape of England itself. By the dawn of the twentieth century, the "green and pleasant land" imagined by William Blake had become wealthy and powerful, but in many places dirty and unhealthy.

PAX BRITANNICA

In 1805, the Royal Navy under Admiral Lord Nelson had decisively defeated the French and Spanish fleets at the Battle of Trafalgar, off the coast of Cadiz, Spain. For the next hundred years, no other power dared challenge the United Kingdom's naval might. The result was that Britain, aided by its wealth from the Industrial Revolution, was able to carve up much of the world in a huge colonial empire. During the 64-year reign (1837–1901) of Queen Victoria, the British Empire spread from Canada to Australia and New Zealand; from Singapore and Hong Kong to Nigeria and South Africa; and above all, across India—the jewel in the imperial Crown. By the time of Queen Victoria's death, about one-quarter of Earth's land surface was controlled from London. The nineteenth century is sometimes called the era of the "Pax Britannica," the peace of Britain, because the world was so dominated by one superpower that no major wars could break out. This is a bit misleading, however, because the British had to fight quite a lot of short, sharp battles against indigenous peoples from Zululand to China who were not always keen on being part of this new empire. But the overwhelming technological advantage that Europeans enjoyed over non-Europeans usually ended the fighting quickly enough. As the English writer Hilaire Belloc put it, with bitter irony:

> *Whatever happens, we have got*
> *The Maxim* gun, and they have not.*
> (* a type of automatic machine gun)

ENGLAND AND THE END OF EMPIRE

Although by 1914 Britain's imperial might looked all-powerful, in fact the United Kingdom was steadily losing ground to industrial rivals such as Germany and the United States. The outbreak of World War I that year signaled the beginning of Britain's long decline. During the war's four terrible years, the British Empire lost a million men, and the country was left with crippling financial debts. During the war, a rebellion broke out in Dublin, Ireland, and though it was quickly suppressed, the political mood in Ireland afterwards was so hostile that in 1921 the British government agreed to allow the southern part of the country to withdraw from the United Kingdom. During the 1920s and 1930s, Britain's worldwide commitments actually grew larger, but it now had much less money with which to meet them. The rise of dictatorships in Germany, Italy, and Japan meant new danger. In 1939, Nazi Germany attacked Poland, and Britain and France consequently declared war on Hitler's Third Reich. The following year, Germany conquered France in a startling six-week victory and was on the brink of invading England. Only the heroism of the Royal Air Force pilots in the 1940 Battle of Britain and the fortitude of Britain's wartime prime minister, Sir Winston Churchill, prevented complete defeat at the hands of the Nazis.

In due course, the Soviet Union and the United States entered the war against Germany, and by 1945, the Axis powers had been defeated. But the United Kingdom was now virtually bankrupt and unable to maintain its worldwide empire. Two years after the war's end, India was granted independence, and throughout the following two decades, most of the rest of the former British Empire peacefully followed suit.

Britain and most of the countries of its former empire formed a mutual association known initially as the British Commonwealth to promote development, education, and matters of joint interest between them. Today, the commonwealth's 1.8 billion citizens, about 30 percent of the world's population, are drawn from the broadest range of faiths, races, cultures, and traditions, and come from 54 independent states. Although its political influence is limited, its aims are to foster international peace and security, democracy, liberty of the individual, and equal rights for all. It also works to eradicate poverty, ignorance, disease, and racial discrimination.

By the 1960s, Britain had recovered somewhat from the worst effects of the war, and living conditions for ordinary people have continued to improve, thanks in part to the extensive postwar welfare state. It was clear, though, that the days of empire and imperial glory were now past. In an odd return to its roots, England was once again becoming a small kingdom off the northwest coast of Europe such as that which Athelstan had ruled a thousand years earlier. Now, however, it was an international power to be reckoned with.

CHAPTER

4

People and Culture

Author and journalist George Orwell once wrote, "When you come back to England from any foreign country, you have immediately the sensation of breathing a different air. The crowds in the big towns, with their mild knobby faces, their bad teeth and gentle manners, are different from a European crowd." Orwell's point about the uniqueness of England and its people is something that many observers have remarked upon over the centuries. It is strange perhaps that a country that has not existed for almost 300 years (since the Act of Union between England and Scotland in 1707, which transformed them both into Great Britain) still retains such obvious distinctive qualities. But the English have not remained unchanged. The influence of nineteenth-century industrialization and its eventual decline, war, and the weakening of old class and religious ties have all had a profound influence on English life and manners. So has immigration to the British Empire and emigration from it. But there remains a lingering sense of England's continuity through time. As Orwell put it: "It is somehow bound up with solid breakfasts and gloomy Sundays, smoky towns and winding roads, green fields and red pillar boxes. It stretches into the future and the past, there is something in it that persists, as in a living creature."

SETTLEMENT PATTERNS AND EARLY IMMIGRATION

Humans have lived in England for at least half a million years. Throughout its early history, settlers traveled from many directions—westward across the North Sea from Germany and Scandinavia, northward from what is now France, southward from Scotland, even eastward from Ireland. It is not always clear whether the new cultures that successively appeared in England up until 1066—Windmill Hill, Beaker, Celtic, Roman, Anglo-Saxon, Viking, Norman—always involved a physical change in population, or simply represent the influence of new ideas and languages. In most cases it was probably a combination of both. Invasions from abroad often meant the dispersal of old communities and the arrival of foreign immigrants. And many local inhabitants may have been assimilated into arriving cultures to "become," say, Roman or Viking. The modern science of genetics, which uses DNA evidence to trace ancestry, has made some interesting discoveries related to this theory. In 1997, for example, scientists proved that a schoolteacher living in the town of Cheddar in Somerset was directly related to a 9,000-year-old man whose skeleton was discovered in a cave just half a mile away from his descendant's home!

After the Norman Conquest in the eleventh century, there were fewer mass influxes of new people to England. However, smaller groups of immigrants continued to arrive, such as German merchants, Dutch textile workers, and French Huguenot (Protestant) refugees from the staunchly Catholic kingdom of Louis XIV. Before the mid-1700s, the population remained relatively small by European standards, at around 5 million people. These were mostly concentrated in small farming communities in southern England. London was the country's only really large city.

All this changed about 250 years ago with the introduction of more efficient agricultural techniques and the beginning of the Industrial Revolution. By 1811, England's population had doubled to 10 million, and by the 1860s, it had quadrupled; at the turn of the twentieth century, 35 million people lived in England. This was not only the result of increased birth- and lowered death rates, but also of huge emigrations from other parts of the British Isles, especially Ireland, which was ravaged by famine in the mid-nineteenth century (today about 800,000 people in England can trace their ancestry to Ireland). The increase is even more surprising when you consider that millions of English men and women were leaving the country at the same time to settle in North America and other parts of the British Empire. The distribution of population altered drastically, as enormous industrial cities sprang up in northern and central England. Most people abandoned the countryside for the towns in search of factory work. During the twentieth century, some of these changes reversed themselves, reflecting the decline of industrialization. Economic depressions reduced the populations of the big northern cities, such as Newcastle and Liverpool, and southern England again became the focus of demographic growth. This was especially true of Greater London, which had a population of about 7.5 million in 2007.

England continues to be an extremely urbanized society. In 2007, more than 90 percent of the population lived in a city or a suburban area. The country's population density is also extremely high, at 930 persons per square mile (360 per square kilometer). Within Europe, only the tiny Netherlands is as tightly packed as England. In 2007, the population of the United Kingdom was estimated at approximately 61 million people, about 50 million of whom live in England. To put this into perspective, England is a country about the size of

In 2007, more than 90 percent of England's population lived in urban or suburban locations. Scenes such as this one, where shoppers make their way down London's Oxford Street, are common in England's urban areas.

Alabama but with the population of New York *and* California combined. However, the population has not increased all that much since the 1960s, reflecting a very significant slowdown in the birthrate from the hectic growth spurts of the nineteenth century. Like many European countries, England is now barely at replacement level. In other words, there are scarcely enough births to keep the population from falling, excluding the effects of immigration. This also means that the national age distribution is changing rapidly, with more elderly people relative to young. Such a disparity may create economic problems in the future, as a dwindling workforce attempts to support an ever-increasing retirement generation.

THE "NEW COMMONWEALTH" BRITISH

One of the most significant changes in England's population structure has been the emigration of non-Europeans from the "New Commonwealth" nations of the Caribbean, Africa, and South Asia, all of whom began arriving in large numbers for the first time after World War II. These immigrants were initially encouraged to come to Britain because of a shortfall in the native manpower pool. However, during the 1960s, increasing resentment of the new Britons pushed the government to enact tougher immigration policies. Unfortunately, racial discrimination and ethnically inspired violence were prevalent in some towns with large nonwhite populations, and this culminated in a series of violent urban riots in the early 1980s. Insensitive and racially prejudiced policing in some large cities was blamed for some of this trouble.

In 2001, there were serious disturbances in the town of Oldham, Lancashire, because of racial fighting between Asian and white teenage gangs. A small political movement called the British National Party (BNP), which opposes nonwhite immigration, made inroads in places such as Oldham as a result. Immigration continues to be a very controversial issue, partly because of the large number of refugees from the Middle East and from African countries such as Somalia. Many people from these lands have sought asylum in England, often entering the country illegally.

Compounding existing racial tensions were the terrorist attacks by suicide bombers who supported Al-Qaeda on the London Underground (subway system) in July 2005. The four bombers caused the deaths of 52 people traveling to work. This was seen by many as the British equivalent of the 9/11 attacks in New York City and Washington, D.C., although a far smaller number of innocent people were killed. At first it was assumed that the terrorists had entered the United Kingdom from abroad, but it was soon established that most of the bombers were British Asian men from England's Muslim community. Three of the four men behind the 2005 suicide bombings were born and raised in England and the other was a Jamaican-born British resident. Consequently, there has been much concern about the activity of Muslim extremists in Britain who have been involved in, or are supportive of, such terrorist acts.

Two weeks after this outrage, on July 21, there were further suicide bomber attacks on the London Underground. This time, mercifully, the bombs all failed to detonate since the explosives had been incorrectly packed, and no one, not even any of the bombers, was killed. Six men have now been charged with this unsuccessful attempt. Since July 2005, there have been further arrests by the police of other suspected terrorists, including those charged with planning equally horrific attacks on airliners crossing the Atlantic from Britain.

Some may feel it is harsh to include this reference to terrorism in this section on the New Commonwealth British, but it is certainly relevant to race relations and to attitudes on immigration. Obviously, most of the New Commonwealth British are peaceful and law-abiding citizens. But attitudes toward immigration are severely influenced by such events. Unfortunately, a small but significant number of the Muslim community—about 6 percent, most of whom are originally from Pakistan—support the *jihadists* and believe their acts were fully justified.

Today, immigration into Britain is seen as one of the major concerns of the British electorate. According to a BBC report in September 2005, immigration made up more than half of Britain's population growth from 1991 to 2001. Successive administrations have seemingly allowed ever-increasing numbers of immigrants into Britain and not just from the New Commonwealth. Illegal immigrants whose applications for entry have been rejected often manage to stay anyway. Many of them are "economic" immigrants whose sole reason for coming is to avail themselves of the generous welfare system and the free National Health Service to which no one is denied access. Quite apart from the enormous strain on the public purse, this heavy influx increases the population density in England, which already ranks among the very highest in Europe. Even established immigrants are often opposed to further immigration at existing levels. They realize that it has a detrimental effect on the quality of life in this small country and especially in the large urban centers where most of them reside.

Despite the many problems, race relations in general have improved, and most English people of color have adjusted quite successfully to their adopted country's lifestyle. This is partly the result of conscious assimilation and partly a reflection of the way that England itself has changed because of its New Commonwealth citizens. A black Peer of the Realm now sits in the House of Lords, and many nonwhite British have become established TV personalities. Ethnic foods such as curry have become a fixture of England's national cuisine. Cities such as London are a cosmopolitan tapestry of people, stores, and goods from all across the former empire and elsewhere. Today, an estimated 7 percent of the total U.K. population is nonwhite, most of whom are from the West Indies, India, Pakistan, Bangladesh, Hong Kong, and sub-Saharan Africa. Nevertheless, this small segment has had a significant impact on the national culture.

In recent years, race relations between England's white and nonwhite populations have improved thanks to a more tolerant atmosphere and general acculturation. Here, Prince Charles meets with Muslim students at the Millennium Galleries in Sheffield, England, in 2006, during an exhibit that celebrated Muslim culture.

LANGUAGE

The vast majority of the population speaks English. Some of the New Commonwealth residents are bilingual in Hindi, Urdu, and other Asian languages, but these are unusual exceptions. The massive international success of English—it is the most widespread language in the world, now used on six continents and second only to Mandarin Chinese in the absolute number of native speakers—has been both a blessing and a curse to its original speakers. Its universality makes it much easier for English goods and services to travel across global frontiers, and the language's literature and ideas have had an incalculable influence on people everywhere. However, this very ease of use has discouraged English people from learning foreign languages, which can be a disadvantage in dealings with, for example, other members of the European Union. Also, English as spoken in Great Britain is now only one subcategory of the language—sometimes called "British English" to distinguish it from other sorts—and is not even the most popular variety, given the rise of the influence of the United States. Sometimes the English feel that they have had their own language stolen away from them.

What those who do not speak it call a "posh" English accent, and those who do an "educated" accent, is spoken mostly in southern parts of England. This does not mean that an "educated" English accent is not sometimes combined with a slight regional dialect. The accent is sometimes called "BBC English" for the national broadcasting organization that once encouraged its use, but apparently does not do so any longer.

Elsewhere in England, people use a dizzying array of regional dialects and accents, many of which are almost incomprehensible to outsiders. Among the most famous are Cockney, spoken in London; Scouse, from Liverpool; Geordie, from Newcastle and Tyneside; and Brummie, from the Birmingham area. The biggest overall difference is between northern and southern varieties of English. Northerners tend to use shorter vowel sounds, for example pronouncing the "a" in the word "bath" in the same way as "fat"; southerners would pronounce it like the "a" in "father." In recent years, the distinctive branches of southern accent have started to be overtaken by a generic London-based dialect known as "Estuary English," loosely based on Cockney. Quite apart from all these homegrown dialects, England has now become so cosmopolitan that one is equally likely to hear Irish and Scottish accents, Indian and West Indian accents, and a whole multitude of other foreign accents in English that is spoken in any city in Britain and even the countryside.

In British English, words are frequently spelled or used differently from the American version of the language. Some U.S. words ending in "or" are written by the British with "our," such as "colour" and "flavour," for instance. Words such as center, sceptre and liter are written as "centre," "scepter," and "litre" in British English. A faucet is a "tap," a vacation is a "holiday," an elevator is a "lift," and so on. An American who wants to check under the hood of his station wagon while pumping gas will be out of luck in England, although he could always take a look under the bonnet of his estate car while getting petrol at the garage!

RELIGION

Unlike the United States, England has an official state religion. The queen is the supreme head of the Church of England, a Protestant Christian faith also known as "Anglicanism" (equivalent to the Episcopal Church in North America). Because of its official nature, the Church of England has some unusual legal rights and responsibilities. The monarch appoints its entire senior clergy, although this task is usually delegated to the prime minister, and, at least until the recent reforms of the House of Lords, its bishops had permanent seats in Parliament. The Church's leader after the queen, the archbishop of Canterbury, crowns the monarch at his or her coronation and is traditionally seen as being charged with the nation's moral and spiritual well-being. An Act of Parliament is required to make any major changes to the Church's constitution. Despite all this, however, the Anglican Church receives no money from the state, and regardless of its large landholdings, the Church today is suffering from serious financial problems because of the number of ancient and increasingly decrepit places of worship under its care. A sharp decline in its active membership has only increased its problems. Anglicanism is a moderate form of Protestantism in which priests have a large amount of discretion about how they conduct their services; the main distinction is between "Low" Church practices, which are similar to Methodism, and "High" Church, which is largely indistinguishable from Catholicism.

Until the mid-nineteenth century, Roman Catholics were ineligible to join many of the important institutions of English life, including Parliament and the universities of Oxford and Cambridge. They achieved freedom of worship in the Victorian period, although no significant Catholic community existed until the influx of Irish immigrants at around the same time. Today, English Catholics are fully integrated into national society, and the only trace of the old restrictions is in the choice of monarch; by law, no king or queen of England can be, or marry, a Catholic. Other important Christian sects that began or developed in England include Methodist, Baptist, Quaker, and Pentecostal, and these communities still exist today.

According to 1995 figures, 43 percent of the U.K. population is Anglican, nearly 10 percent Catholic, and 10 percent part of another Protestant or Greek Orthodox denomination. Does this mean, then, that Britain is a Christian country? Well, yes and no. Attendance figures at regular church services of all types have plummeted in recent years. Fewer than 2 million people are regular communicants at Anglican churches, and there are about the same number of practicing Catholics. The United Kingdom is a much more secular country than the United States, with nearly a third of the population expressing no particular religious faith at all and even those who are nominally members of a church rarely taking part in its services. No amount of promotion on the part of religious leaders seems to be able to budge this spiritual indifference. On the other hand, most Britons still see traditional Christian values as important. And most "Christians" continue to affirm a belief in God, however vaguely this is sometimes expressed. Formal Christianity has declined enormously, as in the rest of Europe, but a lingering sense of the Church's ethical ideals remains.

Although their numbers are relatively small, the non-Christian faiths in England are in some ways much more vibrant. Because the United Kingdom was a sanctuary from Nazi persecutions during World War II, it now has the second-largest Jewish population in Europe. There are about 300,000 Jews living in England, mostly Orthodox in background and predominantly based in the London area. The New Commonwealth immigrants from South Asia brought with them their Islamic, Hindu, and Sikh traditions, and the English Muslim community is especially strong with about one million regular attendees at mosques. It is estimated that there may soon be more practicing Muslims in England than Christians. Occasional controversies have broken out in recent years because of clashes between traditional Islamic belief and the more permissive attitudes of secular Britain. As already mentioned, the terrorist activities of some Muslim extremists in England have caused a considerable polarization of attitudes both within and outside of the Muslim community since the 2005 attacks in London. Polls show that as many as 40 percent of British Muslims would like to see elements of Islamic *Sharia* law incorporated into the laws of Britain.

CLASS

England was traditionally one of the world's most class-conscious countries. Its population used to be clearly divided into social strata that could be recognized by dress, speech, behavior, and attitudes. Someone was born working, middle, or upper class, and remained part of that group from cradle to grave. That, at least, was the old stereotype. Up until about 50 years ago, it remained a fairly accurate description of the way England's social structure was arranged. Class distinctions remained extremely rigid, and it was next to impossible to progress from one to another, even with money, mainly because of the crucial differences in accent. "The English people are branded on the tongue," said George Orwell in the 1940s, by which he meant that the language someone used always gave away their social origins. Power remained very much in the hands of people from well-to-do backgrounds, who attended the private schools and universities.

The slow fading away of these distinctions had several causes. As the British economy shifted away from manufacturing to service industries, more clerical and "white-collar" jobs became available and so the ranks of the middle class grew larger. Educational opportunities at all levels improved, and attendance at the universities of Oxford or Cambridge was no longer the exclusive province of the well born. Even sports and entertainment celebrities played their role by showing how birth was not a barrier to success—if the working-class Beatles from Liverpool could conquer the world in the 1960s, why couldn't other Britons from humble backgrounds also accomplish their dreams? The result was a steady decline in the importance of background or class as an indicator of a person's future prospects and opportunities.

As a result of these societal changes, there have been several academic studies on social mobility—the likelihood that someone from the working class can achieve middle class or upper class status. According to research data, social mobility in England has been increasing over the last 100 years, meaning that a person's class and upbringing are becoming less important in determining future opportunities. Part of the reason for a more open English society is an expanding upper class, allowing more room at the top for others coming from lower socioeconomic classes. The other part of the reason is equal opportunity hiring: The chances of an upper-class man being hired over a working-class man for an upper-class job have steadily decreased, from 10 times as likely in 1900 to 7.7 times as likely in 1960. This is a great improvement over a short period of time, and demonstrates the progess that English society is making towards becoming less class conscious.

ENGLISHMEN AND WOMEN WHO CHANGED THE WORLD

There have been many famous English men and women, but here we will mention just a few whose influence has reached far beyond the shores of England. Necessarily our selection must be limited and so we will exclude monarchs and statesmen and military leaders whose influence has been considerable and look more at those who have changed our outlook and the way we think.

Already we have mentioned William Shakespeare (1564–1616), the English playwright, poet, and actor who is regarded by many literary experts as the greatest English writer of all time. His influence on the theater in the English-speaking world, not to mention literature, has been immense and continues until this day. Adding to his legend is the great sense of mystery that surrounds him. Volumes have been written posing the question: "Who was Shakespeare?" Many have been unable to accept the fact that the Bard came from an ordinary family in Stratford and was neither rich nor particularly well educated.

Not long after Shakespeare's death, another genius of an entirely different sort was born in Lincolnshire and his ideas revolutionized our understanding of the physical world. This was Sir Isaac Newton, the scientist and mathematician who was the first to propose the Theory of Gravitation, which he published in 1684. This finally explained to a high degree of accuracy the motion of the planets around the sun in our solar system, and in particular the movement of the earth in its orbit around the sun, and that of the moon around the earth.

One of England's most famous native sons is William Shakespeare, who many regard as the greatest English writer of all time. During his life, many of Shakespeare's plays were performed at the Globe Theater, which was built in 1599, in the Southwark area of London. Pictured here is a replica of the theater, which opened in 1997 and is known as "Shakespeare's Globe Theatre."

His greatest work, *Philosophiae Naturalis Principia Mathematica* (1687), formulated all of this more rigorously and also proposed his famous Laws of Motion. Thus was born the extremely important subdivision of physics known as

"Dynamics." He also made important discoveries in the field of optical science, publishing a volume entitled *Opticks*, which described, among other things, how white light can be divided into the colors of the rainbow using a prism and the law of refraction which governs this. He also invented the reflecting telescope. Apart from Newton, no one was able to offer such deep insights into the physical workings of the universe until Albert Einstein, who was from Germany, in the twentieth century.

Another English man of science who deserves mention is Michael Faraday (1791–1867), who was a pioneer of electricity. A physicist and chemist, his many discoveries included the laws of electrolysis and electromagnetic induction. From more than 40 years of his research came many of the developments that led to the industrial and domestic use of electricity and its use in lighthouses. He is generally regarded as having been the greatest experimental physicist ever, and there was a time when pupils in England's schools were taught that "Faraday discovered electricity!"

One scientist whose ideas definitely changed our way of thinking was the distinguished naturalist Charles Darwin, who is famous for his Theory of Evolution. From 1831 to 1836, he served aboard HMS *Beagle* as naturalist on a scientific expedition around the world. In the Galapagos Islands in the Pacific Ocean, he observed many variations among the species of plants and animals that he had seen in South America. After much consideration of these matters, he proposed that animal species, including humans, develop over time from common origins by a process of natural selection. Thus, the stronger, fitter, and cleverer are always more likely to predominate with regard to breeding and so positive genetic traits are strengthened and propagated within a particular species. This cast new light on the processes that led to diversification in nature, but it also ran counter to the teachings of Christianity. Consequently, Darwin met much opposition during his lifetime, but the importance of his ideas was recognized and he is still held in the greatest esteem today.

Even in recent times there are many famous scientists of note, and one Nobel Laureate who should not be left out is Francis Crick who, together with U.S. scientist James Watson, discovered the double-helix structure of the DNA molecule in 1953.

So many names spring to mind in the field of English literature that it is difficult to select just a few. Certainly the writer Charles Dickens should be included. His novels are a rich tapestry of social life in England during Victorian times. The scenes depicted were largely based on personal observation and experience and they are rendered with sharp perception. No other writer seems to have had such concern for the anguish, injustice, and social deprivation of the characters he describes, and yet these are presented with humor as well as with sympathy.

Other English writers one should mention include Geoffrey Chaucer, William Blake, Samuel Pepys, John Dunne, John Keats, Emily Brontë, Lewis Carroll, Jane Austen, Lord Byron, Thomas Hardy, Alfred Lord Tennyson, Robert Browning, D. H. Lawrence, Aldous Huxley, George Orwell, Rudyard Kipling, Winston Churchill, and Daphne du Maurier.

There are also many English artists, who may not have changed the world, but whose fame and skill carried their reputation well beyond England. On a shortlist one would probably include John Constable, Thomas Gainsborough, William Hogarth, Sir Joshua Reynolds, George Stubbs, J. M. W. Turner, John William Waterhouse, the sculptor Henry Moore, and David Hockney.

When it comes to notable actors and actresses of English origin, many names will be familiar in the United States and other countries, and the list is long. To name but a dozen, there would be Charlie Chaplin, Cary Grant, Elizabeth Taylor, David Niven, Charles Laughton, Julie Andrews, Peter Sellers, Audrey Hepburn, Sir Laurence Olivier, Hugh Grant, Roger Moore, and Ralph Fiennes. And what movie buff is not familiar with the name of producer and director Alfred Hitchcock?

This section would be incomplete without some mention of composers, musicians, singers, and bands, and again the roll call of internationally acclaimed English stars would be considerable. Perhaps we can leave it by saying—who has not heard of The Beatles and the Rolling Stones?

Also, if we were to extend the term *Englishmen* to those who were of English descent, we could include George Washington, the first president of the United States and often referred to as the "Father of his Country." His forebears came from Sulgrave Manor in Northamptonshire, and it was his great-grandfather John Washington who sailed from England to Virginia in 1656, just 120 years before the American Declaration of Independence.

5

Government and Politics

The United Kingdom, of which England is a part, is unique among major world nations in having no written constitution. That does not mean to say that the country has no constitution at all; in fact, it has one of the oldest in the world. But it is not embodied in a single, formal document, such as the Constitution of the United States of America. Rather, it is a collection of laws and statutes, some official and some binding through the power of tradition and precedent. Although this might sound haphazard—and some Britons would agree that it is—it also has given the United Kingdom an unusual political stability, and its citizens have long enjoyed important civil liberties. England was one of the first modern countries in the world to give serious thought to democratic ideas and the rule of law. Many of the principles enshrined in the U.S. Constitution, such as the "separation of powers" between different branches of government, have their origins in the unwritten U.K. constitution. The informal nature of British law also allows it to be flexible in response to change. Although some of the branches of government have apparently remained the same for centuries, such as the monarchy, their real functions have changed beyond recognition.

THE MONARCHY

The British head of state, the supreme source of all political authority, is the monarch. Since 1952, that has been Queen Elizabeth II of the House of Windsor. As a child, Queen Elizabeth never expected to become monarch. Her father, the duke of York, was only second in line to the throne after his elder brother Edward, the prince of Wales. But in 1936, Edward VIII, as he had become, abdicated his position after less than a year because of his wish to marry an American divorcee, Wallis Simpson—an unpardonable act in those days. Elizabeth's father became king instead, reigning as George VI. King George was greatly respected by the British people for his courage during World War II, but the stress of unexpected public office and illness caused by his heavy smoking was too much for him and he died relatively young. His eldest daughter, Elizabeth, who was only 26 at the time of her father's death, was crowned queen in a spectacular 1953 coronation ceremony that was broadcast throughout the world using the new technology of television. She has reigned ever since. In 2002, she marked her fiftieth year on the throne, her "Golden Jubilee."

In theory at least, the queen's powers are vast. She is the leader of all three branches of government (the executive, the legislature, and the judiciary), commander-in-chief of the armed forces, and head of the Church of England. All public officeholders and civil servants—including soldiers, sailors, and airmen—give a personal oath of loyalty to her. No law can be passed without her consent, and any important decision such as a declaration of war against another country must be made in her name alone. In earlier times, these powers were quite real, and the monarch ruled almost unchecked by any constraint. In practice, however, the history of the British monarchy over the past several hundred years has been the steady reduction of its real decision-making role. Nowadays the queen's influence is mainly nominal, and all genuine authority in the United Kingdom resides with the prime minister and his parliamentary government using "Crown Prerogative," meaning power exercised in the name of the queen.

This is not to say that the queen is irrelevant. She is the physical embodiment of British law and government and is viewed as a vital symbol of the nation's stability. Her presence can be seen everywhere in British life; her image adorns every coin, banknote, and stamp, and her royal coat of arms (with the Norman French motto *Honi Soit Qui Mal Y Pense*—"Shame on Him Who Thinks Evil of It") is displayed on thousands of public buildings. Queen Elizabeth opens every session of Parliament and reads "the Queen's Speech," which is a statement of the government's policy intentions, but is really written by the prime minister. She is also the patron of hundreds of charitable organizations, and makes ceremonial visits both throughout the United Kingdom and often to the Commonwealth countries. She hosts regular garden parties at her official London home (Buckingham Palace) and other royal residences to honor special invited guests. She also has a separate role as the head of the Commonwealth of Nations (as the former British Commonwealth is more formally known), the international organization whose member states are countries from the old British Empire. Queen Elizabeth has been an extremely hardworking and devoted monarch. Although there are some questions about the future of the institution, she personally is widely admired in her own country as well as throughout the world.

PARLIAMENT

The British parliament is also centuries old. Its origin is traced to the 1215 Magna Carta, an agreement that forced King John (of Robin Hood fame) to listen to advice from his barons

After fire destroyed the original Palace of Westminster in 1834, it was rebuilt in the mid-1800s to serve as the new home of the House of Commons and House of Lords. The building, known as the House of Parliament, is pictured here from the south bank of the River Thames, with the famous clock tower "Big Ben" to its right.

before making important political decisions. By the thirteenth century, English kings would summon parliaments together in order to pass new taxes, but only on special occasions. Parliament did not sit as a regular branch of government until the early seventeenth century, when it became the focus of a long-running battle with the king that ultimately led to the Civil War and the Glorious Revolution. After William of Orange succeeded to the throne in 1688, it was recognized that Parliament, not the monarch, would now be the real center of government. Even so, it was not until the twentieth century that kings and queens finally abandoned their pretenses to power.

Parliament is located in the Palace of Westminster, by the River Thames in the center of London. The modern building, with its famous clock tower containing the huge bell known as "Big Ben," was constructed in the mid-nineteenth century after the original was destroyed by fire. Parliament is made up of two houses, the House of Commons and the House of Lords. The House of Commons is the main debating chamber, where laws are passed and crucial issues of the day are discussed. Its members are known as "MPs," or Members of Parliament; as of 2006, there were 646 of them, each representing a regional constituency in England, Scotland, Wales, or Northern Ireland. Nearly all MPs are members of a political party, and usually the largest single party in the House becomes the government, with its leader elected prime minister. The prime minister, who lives at a special government residence called 10 Downing Street, assembles a group of senior MPs from his or her own party to become ministers in his or her government. This select group is known as the cabinet. One of the unique features of the British constitutional system is that the prime minister and his cabinet, sometimes known as the executive (or the day-to-day policy) branch of the state, are also part of the legislative or lawmaking branch. It is as if the U.S. president was also an ordinary congressional representative as well the occupant of the White House. Although this might sound odd, in practice this system works efficiently enough. This means that other MPs, from both government and opposition parties, may put questions to the prime minister in the House of Commons during sessions specifically intended for this purpose.

The House of Lords has gone through extensive changes in the last few years, and at the time of writing its future is still unclear. Traditionally, it is the seat of the "Lords Temporal" and the "Lords Spiritual"—meaning the titled hereditary aristocrats of the realm and the bishops of the Church of England. It is also the House where the "Law Lords," the heads of the judicial branch of government, sit. The House of Lords—commonly called "the Lords"—used to have many of the same powers as the House of Commons, but since the early twentieth century, its authority has been steadily diminishing. In 1911, the so-called Parliament Act removed the Lords' ability to veto new laws. More recently, the Lords has been criticized for being an undemocratic institution that rewards wealth and status with power. As a result, in 1999, the hereditary "Peers of the Realm," as most Lords members are known, lost their automatic right to sit and vote there. The present government has been considering a plan to completely restructure the Lords and turn it into an elected chamber, such as the House of Commons, but the future of such changes is still uncertain.

POLITICAL PARTIES

At least once every five years, the House of Commons is adjourned, and its MPs have to stand for reelection in a general election. This is a time of great political excitement in the United Kingdom, and each political party vies to get as large a percentage of the popular vote as it can. All British citizens older than the age of 18 can vote in the constituency in which they live. There is no separate voting procedure for the executive branch; the prime minister has to be reelected by his constituency residents, just like any other MP. It is even possible, though rare, for an important party member to lose his parliamentary seat and thus be ineligible to take part in government even if his own side wins the election as a whole.

Currently there are three major political parties represented in the House of Commons. The party that won a third term in office in the 2005 general election was the

In 1997, Labour Party leader Tony Blair was elected prime minister of the United Kingdom, defeating Conservative Party incumbent John Major in one of the biggest landslides in British political history. Blair is pictured here at the House of Commons during the Questions to the Prime Minister, a weekly half-hour session during which Members of Parliament ask the prime minister policy questions. In June 2007, he was succeeded by his colleague Gordon Brown (seen right).

Labour Party, under Prime Minister Tony Blair. The result gave Labour 356 of the 646 seats in the House of Commons and an overall majority of 66. This was despite polling only 35.3 percent of the popular vote, equating to approximately 22 percent of the electorate based on the estimated turnout of 61.3 percent. This majority was far lower than Labour's

163-seat majority in the previous general election (2001) and this was attributed to the electorate's disillusionment with the government and Tony Blair in particular. This breakdown in trust led many who had previously voted Labour to vote for the opposition parties. The loss of confidence in Prime Minister Tony Blair, both in his own Labour Party and outside it, has largely been due to his commitment to the 2003 invasion and the subsequent war in Iraq. The large-scale failure of the American and British peacekeeping forces in Iraq to produce stability and democracy in that country and the ever-mounting death toll among British troops there and in Afghanistan has cost him much of his previous popularity. On June 27, 2007, Blair stepped down as prime minister and handed over this office to his colleague, then Chancellor of the Exchequer, Gordon Brown.

The Labour Party is more than 100 years old and was formed by trade union representatives to give working-class voters a voice in Parliament. Traditionally, the Labour Party has adopted left-wing socialist policies; it was Labour that introduced the extensive welfare state system after its parliamentary victory in 1945. However, after a series of electoral disasters in the 1980s and early 1990s, Labour's leadership slowly eased the party toward the political center. It reduced its involvement with the trade unions and dropped a number of increasingly unpopular proposals to nationalize important parts of the British economy. Tony Blair, in presenting himself and his policies as "New Labour," was successful in returning Labour to power. Nonetheless, critics within his own party complain that in seeking electoral success he abandoned many of the principles on which the Labour movement was originally based. Such socialist attitudes echo old Marxist doctrines, now discredited since the fall of Communism, that still resurface in today's Labour Party. They are evident in the often strident anti-Americanism and opposition to the close alliance Blair formed with U.S. president George W. Bush.

The second-largest party after the 2005 election, with 198 MPs, was the Conservative Party—sometimes known as the "Tories." Conservatives, who as their name implies take a more cautious, right-of-center attitude toward issues, were the party of government throughout much of the twentieth century. In 1979, their leader, Margaret Thatcher, became the country's first female prime minister, an office she held for 11 years. This made her the longest-serving prime minister for more than 150 years. Thatcher, known as the "Iron Lady," remains a controversial figure. After her first term of office, she returned with a landslide majority in 1983. She made many important structural changes to British industry and so brought about a revival of the United Kingdom's flagging economy. Still, opponents accused her of trying to crush the trade unions and destroy the welfare state. Her government followed a radical program of privatization and deregulation, reform of the trade unions, tax cuts, and the introduction of market mechanisms into health and education. The aim was to reduce the role of government and increase individual self-reliance.

During the 1980s, she became a well-known figure on the international scene, striking up a famous friendship with U.S. president Ronald Reagan and winning praise from Soviet leader Mikhail Gorbachev. After her resignation in 1990, the new Conservative leader, John Major, became prime minister. Major was a less colorful figure than Thatcher, but internal differences in his party over U.K. membership of the European Union caused havoc for his administration. He suffered a humiliating defeat at the hands of Tony Blair in the general election of 1997.

The Liberal Democratic Party came in third in the 2005 election with 62 MPs. "Lib-Dems," as they are sometimes known, have a complex history. The old Liberal Party was a powerful force in British politics up to World War I, when it went into a long, slow decline. In the early 1980s, it was joined by a group of breakaway Labour MPs who were unhappy with their party's increasingly left-wing stance. This parliamentary alliance eventually resulted in the founding of a new party. Today, the Liberal Democrats campaign for stronger pro-European links, and they are equally committed to reforming the existing voting system, which, they argue, discriminates against smaller parties such as themselves.

ENGLISH REGIONAL GOVERNMENT

While all the regions of the United Kingdom are represented similarly in Westminster, each has its own unique form of local government providing for police forces, fire brigades, health care, education, and so on. England is no exception to this. The English system is a rather intricate product of centuries of overlapping laws and traditions. As recently as the early 1970s, much of England was still governed by administrative units dating back to the Anglo-Saxons and the Normans. The three main bodies were, in increasing order of size, the parish, the borough, and the county (or shire). Parishes were small church districts, usually centered on a town or village, which originally had a responsibility to provide welfare to old and poor residents. They, in turn, were organized into boroughs, both rural and urban, which had their own courts of law and local government officials. During the nineteenth century, borough councils developed with elected representatives. Finally there were the 40 shire counties, some extremely big, such as Yorkshire (which was so large that it was subdivided into three "ridings," north, east, and west), and some tiny, such as Rutland or Huntingdonshire. The monarch's personal representatives in each county were the lord lieutenants, and also the high sheriffs, whose jobs were to enforce the sovereign's law.

Parishes, boroughs, and counties all continue to exist. But the local government reorganization of 1974 changed many of their boundaries and functions. Some of the historic counties, such as

Westmoreland and Rutland vanished, while new ones such as Humberside and Cumbria appeared. Metropolitan counties, representing large urban units, such as Manchester and Birmingham, were created. These changes remain controversial to this day, and there has been much tinkering with the system since the 1970s. The biggest complaint has been over county boundary changes. Counties have always been more than just bland administrative units; they have strong local traditions and inspire a fierce loyalty in their residents, just as states do in the U.S. People born and raised in one county are very unhappy to be told that they now live in another, however "rational" such reorganization might seem from the administrative viewpoint of Westminster.

London has unique arrangements of its own. The original Roman city of London was only one square mile in size, bordered on all sides by a defensive wall. For centuries afterward, this tiny area—known as "the City"—was technically the extent of London's jurisdiction. The City today has virtually no residents, but contains many banks and financial institutions and such landmarks as St. Paul's Cathedral and the Tower of London. Its medieval guilds continue to elect an honorary mayor who has important ceremonial functions, but no real administrative power. As London grew, it became increasingly obvious that these antique provisions were unsatisfactory. A larger county of London was created, but the city continued to expand into the neighboring counties of Middlesex, Kent, and Surrey. In 1963, "Greater London," encompassing more than 7 million people and divided into 32 boroughs, appeared on the map. Twenty-three years later, the Greater London Council was abolished by the government of Margaret Thatcher, leaving the city the only metropolis in the world without any unified city government. This situation changed again in 2000 with the appointment of Greater London's first directly elected mayor, Ken Livingstone.

In 2000, Ken Livingstone (right) was appointed the first mayor of London and was reelected to the post in 2004. The former Labour Party member is pictured here with Queen Elizabeth II and her husband, Prince Philip, the duke of Edinburgh, during the opening of London's new City Hall in 2002.

POLITICAL REFORM?

As illustrated, the British constitution is a sometimes-bewildering assortment of laws and institutions, old and new, with recent innovations alongside thousand-year-old customs. Although there is much continuity to the system, it has always been subject to reform and change. In the seventeenth and eighteenth centuries, Parliament enforced its rights against the power of the monarch. In the Victorian era, the House of Commons was opened up to larger membership, and voting privileges based on property ownership were repealed. During the twentieth century, women also won the right to vote, the influence of the House of Lords was steadily reduced, and local government was reorganized. Now, critics of the United Kingdom's current political arrangements believe that further reforms appropriate to a new century are also required.

In 1977, at the time of Queen Elizabeth's Silver Jubilee, celebrating her twenty-fifth year on the throne, the position of the British monarchy seemed unassailable. Now a small minority of the population has indicated in opinion polls that it would like to see a presidential republic take over after the death of the reigning monarch. There are several reasons for the decline in deference toward the Royal Family, including the controversy that surrounded the late Princess Diana and her failed marriage to Charles, the prince of Wales. Throughout its history, the monarchy's popularity has ebbed and flowed. Just because it is currently going through a troubled period does not necessarily mean that it is doomed. The majority of Britons continue to support the idea of a constitutional monarch, and none of the three major British political parties has an official policy of republicanism. However, there are a few individual MPs, mostly from the Labour Party, who favor abolition of the monarchy.

Westminster's powerful centralized role has also come under fire in recent years, especially from people in Scotland, Wales, and Northern Ireland. They complain that the "British" state is really just the English state under an assumed name, and that England dominates the United Kingdom to their disadvantage. In defense of the current system, some politicians have claimed that this injustice is more mythical than real. The other U.K. regions are overrepresented in the House of Commons by population size, they point out, and non-English citizens tend to receive higher state benefits per person than the English. It is undeniable, however, that Parliament's physical location in London, and the unfortunate tendency by English people to ignore their neighbors' complaints, has caused some resentment. The recent creation of a Scottish parliament in Edinburgh and a Welsh one in Cardiff, in addition to the successful attempt at creating a power-sharing government in Northern Ireland, may allay some of these criticisms for now. But the long-term continuance of the United Kingdom in its present form is by no means guaranteed.

6

England's Economy

The United Kingdom is one of the richest countries in the world. In 2006, its Gross Domestic Product (GDP), a standard measure of national wealth, was estimated at $1.9 trillion, making the United Kingdom one of only four European countries with a GDP of more than US$1 trillion. Britain is a founding member of the "G-8" group of advanced industrial nations that meets periodically to discuss world economic policy. It imports and exports goods and services worth hundreds of billions of dollars every year, and is one of the United States' half-dozen most important trading partners. England, as the largest and most populous region of the United Kingdom, is the main contributor to this financial powerhouse, and its capital city, London, is the focus of England's wealth.

Britain's economic performance has not always been a source of pride, however. In the 1970s, the United Kingdom was sometimes referred to as "the sick man of Europe" because of its flagging production output, high unemployment, and rampant inflation. Some of this was attributable to the stranglehold exercised by organized labor on large sections of British industry that were no longer profitable and which survived only because of government subsidies. This would change during the 1980s, but not without hardship, as a result of reforms by the Conservative Party.

As the world's first industrial nation, Britain was also one of the first countries to undergo the harsh realities of "deindustrialization," as its old manufacturing base was dismantled under the pressure of new foreign competition. The United Kingdom is a good example of what is called a postindustrial nation, a country that has built up and lost its heavy industry and replaced it with a predominantly service-oriented economy. Modern Britain's greatest economic opportunity, but also its biggest dilemma, is its continued role within the European Union (EU), as that organization proceeds with monetary and political unification.

NATURAL RESOURCES

England, at the brink of the Industrial Revolution in the mid-1700s, had the perfect natural resources to create a modern factory-based economy. Its forests of broad-leaved and conifer trees provided an excellent source of timber for the burgeoning shipbuilding industry. And its rock, gravel, and sand quarries, as well as its reserves of clay and salt, were necessary ingredients for the manufacturing industry. Above all, the green fields of England were built on coal—lots of coal. Huge underground reserves in Tyneside, Yorkshire, and Nottinghamshire were mined for their vital "black gold," which powered English steamships across the globe and kept the country's railroads, iron, and steel works running. The city of Newcastle in northeastern England produced and distributed so much coal that the phrase "sending coals to Newcastle" became a stock expression for a pointless activity.

England still has a significant timber and mineral industry, but over the last century it has steadily shrunk in importance as its resources have dwindled and cheaper foreign alternatives have become available. The story of the coal industry is especially sad. As English coal became increasingly uncompetitive on the world market in the 1970s and 1980s, the governments of the day sought to restructure the mining sector and close down the least profitable pits. This provoked a dispute with the powerful National Union of Mineworkers (NUM) that led to a bitter yearlong strike in 1984–1985. Ultimately the government prevailed and most of England's remaining coal mines were closed down during the following decade. This left some mining communities destitute, especially in northern England, and for years this remained a source of resentment among former mineworkers.

Despite the decline in coal production, the United Kingdom continues to be an unusually large producer of energy resources, with about 10 percent of its GDP being energy related—the highest share of any major industrial nation. This is because of the discovery of large oil and natural gas reserves in the North Sea during the 1970s. These oil and gas fields lie under the seabed in what is one of the roughest stretches of water in the world. Extraction requires specially engineered offshore platforms to tap into the rich natural resources below the waves. For months on end, drillers live on these lonely man-made islands pumping oil and gas back to the mainland. North Sea energy has brought in valuable government revenues, but Britain's power needs far exceed what can be extracted from offshore waters. The country remains dependent on imported fuels for most of its electrical power production. Some alternative energy initiatives have been attempted. The world's first commercial atomic power station was opened at Calder Hall in northwestern England in 1956, and the United Kingdom continues to have a string of nuclear reactors as part of its national energy system. Fears about their safety, however, have

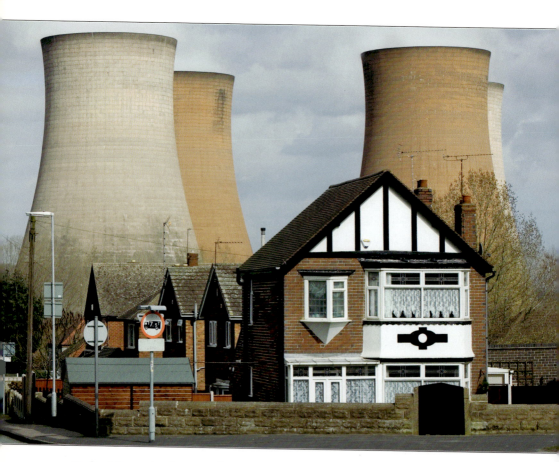

England has several conventional power plants, including Rugeley Power Station, which is located in Staffordshire in the English Midlands. The coal-fired power station opened in 1963 and generates electricity for approximately 1,000,000 people.

discouraged further large-scale investment. Some attempts to utilize solar, wind, and wave power are ongoing, but as yet these have not become important sources of Britain's energy.

AGRICULTURE AND FISHING

One of the most distinctive features of the English landscape, especially when seen from above in an airplane, is the patchwork quilt of irregular fields that covers the countryside. England's farming economy went through an early reorganization from the 1500s onward known as the "Enclosures," and this combined the tiny strips of medieval farmland into larger, more efficient units. But the British never developed the enormous field systems such as those found on the broad prairies of the United States and Canada. And by North American standards, English agriculture is very unevenly organized. This is not to say that it is unproductive. On the contrary, England's farming industry is probably the best organized in Europe, and the country produces 60 percent of its food needs using only one percent of the total labor force. England's fertile lowlands have always been the best part of the United Kingdom for farming, and the introduction of mechanization in the twentieth century made England largely self-reliant in the production of wheat, barley, and potatoes. (Incidentally, one of the confusing concepts for American visitors to understand is that wheat is often referred to as "corn," meaning grain, whereas the English call corn "maize.") Market gardening, or the growing of fruits, flowers, and vegetables, is especially popular in southern England. The county of Kent is traditionally known as the "Garden of England" and is famous for the growing of hops (used in making beer) and for its orchards and flowerbeds. Some parts of the south and southwest are warm enough all the growing season to plant vineyards and bottle wine.

Just as the English sometimes (rather impolitely) call their French neighbors "frogs" because of their reputed taste for frogs legs, so the French have traditionally called the English "Rostbifs" (Roast Beefs). This indicates how important the cattle industry has historically been, not just for England's economy but for the country's whole way of life. In the early 1990s, troubling reports began to emerge that Britain's cow herds were infected with a mysterious, crippling virus known as BSE, or mad cow disease. Even worse, medical evidence showed that in rare circumstances humans could contract a very similar disease (variant CJD), possibly as a result of eating infected beef.

The BSE scare resulted in Britain's beef exports being banned across Europe and North America, and 4.5 million cattle had to be slaughtered to expunge the disease from the country's herds. If this were not bad enough for livestock farmers, in 2001, an equally devastating infection called foot-and-mouth disease broke out in sheep and pig farms across the United Kingdom. The government took drastic action, ordering the slaughter of almost 4 million more animals to prevent the further spread of this infection. These twin disasters have done enormous damage to Britain's livestock industry, and it may take quite some time for the country's farmers to recover.

The recent story of England's fishing industry also is not a happy one. For centuries, deep-sea fishermen based in ports such as Lowestoft, Great Yarmouth, and Grimsby have battled the tempestuous waters of the Atlantic Ocean and the North Sea to bring in the catch of cod, haddock, whiting, and other saltwater fish. Fish has traditionally been an important part of the English diet, and "fish 'n' chips"—battered fish and fries—is a regular choice on the national dinner plate. But overfishing by large mechanized trawlers, in particular those belonging to other European Union member states, has dangerously depleted fish stocks in the seas surrounding the British Isles. Furthermore, rigid EU quotas on the amount of fish that can now be caught every year has made it difficult for fishermen to remain in business. The future of the English fishing industry is very uncertain.

MANUFACTURING AND HEAVY INDUSTRY

In the nineteenth century, Prime Minister Benjamin Disraeli described Britain as the workshop of the world. This was not an idle boast. Britain, by virtue of being the world's first industrialized country, was the single biggest source of all manufacturing and heavy industrial goods. The United Kingdom's products were sold throughout the world, and British inventors dreamed up many of the machines and devices that we take for granted today—the steam engine, railroad, telephone, television, and the computer, to name but a few. Manchester, in northern England, was the world's first industrial city and the model for all subsequent factory-based towns.

By the end of World War II in 1945, many of the country's older industries were feeling the pinch of low productivity and fierce international competition. The postwar Labour Party government nationalized large industries, such as steelmaking, but this did not prevent their long-term decline. In 1979, Margaret Thatcher's Conservative administration came into power and introduced a tough monetary policy that made it very difficult for many of the United Kingdom's older and more inefficient manufacturers to remain in business. Thousands of factory jobs were lost, both in private and state-run industry. Over the next decade, the Thatcher government denationalized much of the United Kingdom's remaining public industries in share sales to members of the public prepared to invest.

Today, England is much less reliant on manufacturing and traditional heavy industry than it was even 20 years ago. Nonetheless, one in five of its workers is still in the manufacturing sector. Those firms that survived the reorganization of the 1980s tended to be in hi-tech areas, such as microelectronics, aircraft production, chemicals, and pharmaceuticals. Older crafts such as brewing, textiles, and paper and glass production still exist, but on a smaller scale. England's shipbuilding, motorbike, and car industries have largely disappeared, although a few highly specialist firms, such as Rolls-Royce, survive because of the prestige of their products.

SERVICES

What has largely replaced manufacturing as the hub of the United Kingdom's economy is the service sector. Services span everything from banking and insurance, to information technology and computer software, to tourism, and from retail to the entertainment industry. About two-thirds of the English

Tourism is one of England's primary sources of revenue: In 2005, the industry generated more than $135 billion. Pictured here are groups of tourists visiting Buckingham Palace in 2006, a year after the terrorist bombings in London killed 52 people. Although the number of tourists declined in the first few months after the bombings, the industry quickly rebounded.

workforce is now part of the service sector, and this proportion continues to grow. London was at one time the world's most important financial center, and "the City" in the capital's business district continues to be a key global marketplace, particularly for dealing in precious metals, such as gold and silver. The London Stock Exchange, founded in 1773, ranks alongside Wall Street and the stock markets of Frankfurt, Hong Kong, and Tokyo as a focus for international share and bond trading. An even older institution is the insurance broker Lloyds, which opened its doors for the first time in 1688 and has been the world's main shipping underwriter for more than three centuries.

Tourism has become one of the United Kingdom's most vital money-earners, with earnings estimated at more than $135 billion in 2005. Around 25 million people visit Britain every year, predominantly from the United States and elsewhere in Europe. Needless to say, catering to this massive influx of guests has become a major task for the national economy. England's part in this annual migration to the United Kingdom is vital, because of the country's large number of sought-after tourist attractions. London, with its historical landmarks, vibrant nightlife, and famous theater traditions is a natural starting point for travelers to the United Kingdom. But every region of England enjoys a rich variety of scenic beauty and sight-seeing opportunities. Homegrown tourism is also important. Traditionally, the English used to like to "be beside the seaside" on their summer vacations and flocked to coastal resorts such as Brighton, Blackpool, and Skegness. The fickleness of the English weather means that these towns cannot compete with Spain or Florida for sunshine, but these and many other seaside resorts remain part of the English vacation experience for the minority who do not go abroad.

No survey of English services would be complete without a mention of the music business. Ever since the so-called British Invasion of the United States in the 1960s by bands such as The Beatles and the Rolling Stones, popular music has been an important national revenue source. Fashions come and go, but English singers and bands continue to do very well abroad, especially in the vital American market. In 2005 and 2006, the Rolling Stones still led the annual list of the U.S. music world's top moneymakers, as published by *Forbes* magazine; in 2006, they earned $150.6 million. So Mick Jagger and his bandmates are still helping to support Britain's balance of trade, although many other groups and singers from England can be said to have contributed to this vital export.

TRANSPORTATION AND TRADE

England is a relatively small country and is well served by a modern transportation network. The three major airports in the London area, Heathrow, Gatwick, and Stansted, together handle more than 40 million passengers each year. In the 1960s, the government began a major road-building program that linked the United Kingdom's cities by motorways (interstates) traversing the country. Car ownership and use is widespread among Britons, and major traffic congestion has become a serious economic as well as environmental problem in recent years. Many urban areas are adopting "pedestrianization," or the closing off of city centers to automobile traffic, as one way of cutting back on the pollution and the frustration caused by too many cars on the road. To encourage travel by other means, some towns have revamped their bus services and discourage private cars from entering city centers by imposing steep parking charges and punitive fines for infringement. Bicycle use also is common, and, in addition to its exercise value, a bike can be a good way of getting around England's complex and narrow city streets.

In 2003, a "London Congestion Charge" was introduced and all motorists entering the Central London area had to pay US$8 a day. (The charge was later raised to US$14 a day.) London is the largest city ever to impose such a charge. CCTV cameras and other license plate recognition technology are used to identify cars whose drivers have failed to pay, resulting in a fine usually in excess of $100. However, Londoners are particularly fortunate in that they can rely on the capital's famous underground, or "tube" train service. The rest of the United Kingdom has a widespread railroad network, but since its privatization in

In 1994, the Channel Tunnel, which connects England and France, opened for business. The 31-mile- (50-kilometer-) long tunnel is the second longest in the world, and the trip takes approximately 20 minutes.

the 1990s, many commuters have complained that the service has deteriorated. Over the years, a number of high-profile train accidents have damaged the industry's reputation for safety both before and after privatization.

Until 1994, the only way to reach Great Britain from abroad was by air or by sea. This changed during that year when the Channel Tunnel between Folkestone on the Kent Coast and

Calais, France, was opened by Queen Elizabeth and the French president, François Mitterand. The Eurotunnel, as it is known officially, provides the first British land bridge to the European mainland since the end of the last ice age. Although both countries had talked about such a tunnel since the nineteenth century, fears of military invasion and the engineering difficulties involved kept all plans strictly on the drawing board until the 1980s. Then an Anglo-French consortium began drilling operations on either side of the English Channel and eventually the main rail tunnels were joined, meeting in the middle in 1991, and opening for business three years later. Even now, many Britons are concerned about the increase in drug smuggling and illegal immigration that the Channel Tunnel is bringing, as well as the possibility of catastrophic terrorist attack.

Trade remains a very important factor in the British economy. In 2006, the United Kingdom imported $603 billion worth of goods and exported $469 billion, chiefly to other European Union members but also to the United States and Japan. The country makes up in part this trade deficit by the "invisible" earnings it receives from financial services, such as banking, stockbroking, and insurance, in the city of London. Dividends from business investments in other countries are also very important in keeping the account books balanced. Throughout the early twentieth century, Britain had the largest merchant marine of any nation, which it used to carry its trade across the world's oceans. Shipping losses in the two world wars and the gradual replacement of sea by air transport whittled away this mighty fleet. Nowadays, relatively few vessels continue to fly the "Red Ensign," although there are still some high-profile ships, such as the luxury liner *Queen Elizabeth II* (known as the *QE2*).

THE EUROPEAN QUESTION

Britain's economic future will be dominated by its relationship with the European Union (EU), which it joined in 1973. The question of the Common Market, as it used to be known, has played a key role in the country's politics for more than 25 years and has dogged the governments of all political parties.

When it was originally established, the EU—then called the EEC, or European Economic Community—was intended to be a free-trade area for western European nations, a means of bringing their national economies together and discouraging the kind of cross-border tensions that had led to the wars of 1914 and 1939. Over time other, more ambitious, goals developed. In 1991, its members signed the Maastricht Agreement, which committed them to a timetable for monetary union by the end of the decade. The United Kingdom was unenthusiastic about this plan and opted to remain out of the single European currency, although it stayed in the EU. This new currency, the *euro*, was unveiled at the beginning of 2002, and now most of the EU's members have adopted it as their national monetary unit. This leaves Britain in a dilemma. The majority of the British public remains unconvinced about the merits of the single currency and many members of Parliament are fiercely opposed to its introduction. On the other hand, if Britain clings to the pound for too long, then the other EU members may become impatient with the United Kingdom's excessive caution and press ahead without the British; they might even demand that Britain leave the European Union. Critics of the EU back in England would be delighted with this result, of course!

Despite much discussion on the subject in 2003 and the prime minister's insistence on keeping open the option of adopting the euro, opinion in many parts of Europe, even in France, was turning against the single currency. A referendum in Sweden firmly rejected adopting the euro, and in the United Kingdom the idea of holding a referendum on the issue became increasingly less attractive in case the public voted like the Swedes. The British government minister responsible for financial affairs, the chancellor of the Exchequer, has laid down certain financial conditions that must be met before he will consider opting for the euro. The outcome will have a decisive effect on the future economic development of the United Kingdom, and it will be fascinating to see whether the government will allow a referendum, or will put this vexing issue on ice for the foreseeable future.

7

Living in England Today

E ngland has experienced the same kind of changes in the makeup of family life as North America during the past 50 years. Older, more traditional forms of extended family, where many generations lived closely together—even under the same roof—gave way to smaller nuclear families with two adult parents and perhaps one or two children. Nuclear families in turn have broken down with the rapid rise in divorce, single parenthood, and living together outside of marriage. Some conservative critics argue that these trends are the result of a permissive society in which too much tolerance toward alternative living styles has resulted in broken homes, juvenile delinquency, and teenage pregnancy. There are indeed many valid concerns about the direction of some English social trends. Violent crime, though much lower than in the United States, has risen dramatically since World War II, while the divorce rate has skyrocketed and the number of young unmarried mothers has increased many times over. However, others claim that these regrettable developments are the inevitable result of more deep-seated economic changes, experienced in all advanced industrial nations, and that in practice there is little that society can do about them. Although there is much alarmism in the national media about the imminent "collapse of civilization," England remains a largely peaceful, law-abiding country with a surprisingly resilient respect for older social customs.

Until 1918, women in England were denied the right to vote (something that was challenged by an extremely noisy and often violent "Suffragette" movement) and had few vocational opportunities other than motherhood, domestic service, and a few niche industries, such as textiles. During the two world wars, women poured into the factories to replace men called up by the army, and their contribution to the war effort left a lasting mark on gender roles. More and more women entered the workforce, including the legal and health professions, in the postwar period. In 1979, when Margaret Thatcher was elected prime minister, the United Kingdom was almost unique in having both a female head of state (the queen) and a female head of government. Despite these high-profile successes, however, many English women still complain that they are underpaid relative to men and that they remain burdened with too many of their traditional household duties during marriage. The lack of good state-subsidized nursery facilities is a bone of contention for younger working women, who are often faced with the dilemma of maintaining their careers or becoming full-time mothers.

HEALTH AND WELFARE

In 1945, a Labour Party government was elected with a mandate from the voters to create Britain's first comprehensive health and social security system, something that became known as the "Welfare State." Before World War II, Britain had been blighted by crippling poverty and unemployment in many depressed industrial areas. There was a determination by the new political class to knock down the urban slums and replace them with better housing and facilities for working people. Postwar local councils built hundreds of thousands of new homes, many of them publicly owned and available to new residents for a low rent. They also embarked on the large-scale construction of high-rise apartment blocks, which unfortunately often became as ill kempt and dangerous as the nineteenth-century slums they had replaced. A national insurance scheme for all workers was introduced. It guaranteed old age and disability pensions, unemployment benefits, and payments for low-earning families to everyone who contributed from their pay-packets. This social security plan remains largely in place today, although it has been much revised to take into account growing costs and the problems of bureaucratic inefficiency. Its enduring popularity with the electorate prevented prime ministers, such as Margaret Thatcher, who was unconvinced about the wisdom of some aspects of the Welfare State, from interfering too much with its structure. However, the changes in the British population's age demographics will make it very difficult to maintain the current system, with regard to pensions in particular, without a drastic increase in funding. More and more elderly people will have to be supported by a relatively shrinking workforce.

Perhaps the most important achievement of the Welfare State reforms was the creation in 1948 of the National Health Service, or NHS. This committed the British state for the first time in history to provide free on-demand health care for the entire population "from cradle to grave," as the saying went. Nothing in this world is really free, of course, and taxpayers had to provide for the cost of the NHS through their national insurance contributions. But the guarantee that medical care would henceforth be provided to ordinary people without considering their ability to pay was a major breakthrough in public health, and one that Britons remain proud of to this day. Like the rest of the Welfare State system, the NHS has had to adapt to changing conditions in the twenty-first century. The expansion of its role as medical science advances and the population ages has put it under great pressure to deliver quality care, and there have been complaints that a service, once envied around the world, has become underfunded, administratively bloated, and inefficient. Private medical care, which is available at an extra cost, has become a more popular option in recent years.

EDUCATION

The third plank of the Welfare State after social security and health was a new education system, actually brought in a little earlier by the wartime Conservative government in 1944. The structure of primary and secondary education in England and Wales—Scotland has its own procedures—has changed often since the war, and remains in flux today. Broadly speaking, the current organization is as follows. All children are required to attend school between the ages of five and sixteen. When they reach age 11, they usually transfer from a primary to a secondary, or "comprehensive," school. In the old system, students took an exam at this point and either qualified to attend a grammar school, with the intention of eventually going to university, or a less academically prestigious secondary-modern school. Nowadays, the two types of school have been combined (a point that still generates much criticism from traditional educators). At the age of 16, pupils take their GCSE, or General Certificate exams. They are free to leave school at this point to find employment, but increasingly many students stay on for another two years in the equivalent of high school, known in England as the "Sixth Form," to take "A" or Advanced level exams. If their A-levels are good enough, then they can go on to college. In recent years, the percentage of students who have passed these exams has risen to unprecedented levels. However, it has become increasingly evident that much of this is due to easier exam questions, rather than any particular rise in the intellectual excellence of the pupils. Some traditional

Established in 1167, the University of Oxford is the oldest university in the English-speaking world. This aerial view of the campus centers on Radcliffe Camera, which was the original location of the Radcliffe Science Library but is now home to the university's History, English, and Theology collection.

educators claim that this policy undermines the whole value of the education system.

The two best-known higher learning institutions in England are the universities of Oxford and Cambridge, founded in 1167 and 1209, respectively. Both are world famous for the quality of education they provide, and students from across the United Kingdom and indeed the globe vie for the opportunity to study there. There are more than 80 other colleges and universities across the United Kingdom, all of which are nominally independent, but in practice (with one exception, the University of Buckingham) rely on state funds. There is also the so-called Open University, which was developed in the 1960s to allow adults to obtain a degree by distance learning. Until the early 1990s, university students received generous government stipends and free tuition to provide for them during their studies. More recently, tuition payments have been levied directly and grants replaced by student loans, although the cost of a good college education in England remains much lower than it is in the United States.

Although a comparatively small number of pupils attend them, a word must be said about England's famous private schools, such as Eton College and Harrow. These prestigious institutions are well known because many former pupils have attained high office, prominence, and celebrity (or in some cases notoriety) status. Confusingly, these fee-charging private schools are known in the United Kingdom as "public schools"—this dates back to the medieval period when most rich families educated their children using private tutors and did not send them away to school. These public schools were, in their way, the first type of national school system available to ordinary middle-class parents. At one time, virtually the whole of England's social and political elite went through this handful of schools, which, despite their high fees, were sometimes run in a cavalier manner. Although their influence has declined somewhat, many ambitious parents still seek to educate their children this way, and it is true that former public schoolboys and girls tend to do well academically and therefore are more likely to win university places. For this reason, some universities, such as Oxford and Cambridge, now discriminate against would-be public school entrants. Because of political correctness, they maintain that, if this was not done, it would be unfair to disadvantaged entrants from working-class backgrounds.

SPORTS AND LEISURE

England is a nation of sports fanatics and is the birthplace of three of the most popular games in the world—soccer, rugby, and cricket. Professional soccer—called football in England—is by the far the best-loved game of all, and hundreds of thousands of fans regularly attend matches that involve England's prestigious teams—Manchester United, Liverpool, Arsenal, and Chelsea. The English national squad has only won the World Cup once, in 1966, and this event is remembered fondly by all soccer-loving citizens. Rugby is a nineteenth-century derivative of soccer in which players are allowed to carry the ball, and it is divided into professional Rugby League and amateur Rugby Union rules. The Six Nations tournament between England, Scotland, Wales, Ireland, France, and Italy is one of the key events on the rugby calendar.

Cricket is not that well known in the United States, but it is enormously popular in England and many parts of the former British Empire, such as India, Pakistan, Australia, New Zealand, and the Caribbean. Its complex rules defy simple explanation, but it is a game similar to baseball in which the object is to pitch (or bowl) the opposing batsman out. Modern English cricket fans take an almost ghoulish pleasure in seeing their national side consistently defeated by other Commonwealth teams.

Other sports that are popular in England include horse racing, snooker (similar to billiards), darts, Grand Prix racing, and tennis, especially the annual international tournament at Wimbledon, near London. One could well have included fox-hunting (on horseback and with a pack of hounds) as a popular country sport, but recent controversial legislation introduced in Parliament in 2005 has banned hunting with dogs in England. That is not to say this sport has come to an end; during 2006,

One of England's most popular sports is cricket, which has been played competitively since the 1600s. In the past century, cricket has arguably become the world's second-most popular sport behind soccer. Pictured here is a match between England and Pakistan during the NatWest One Day International Series in 2006.

foxhunting went on in various parts of the country just as if the law had never been passed.

There are almost as many leisure activities in England as there are people, but some of the better known are freshwater fishing, hiking (or "rambling"), golf, and gardening. Less energetic pursuits include gambling, either at the racetrack or in betting shops, or at one of the more than 100 casinos that have sprung up in England in recent years. In the same category, many Britons try their luck every week with lotto tickets in the

National Lottery. Trips to the local pub, weekend adventures staying at hotels or bed-and-breakfast establishments in the countryside, and, of course, camping round off these popular leisure activities.

The English are renowned for being a nation of eccentric hobbyists, with thousands of weird and wonderful diversions such as crossword puzzles, mystery novels, ballroom dancing, stamp collecting, and train spotting. One of the charms of English life is the rich culture of private enthusiasms that people enjoy either alone or through clubs and societies.

MEDIA AND ENTERTAINMENT

The British Broadcasting Corporation, or BBC, is the principal television and radio company in the United Kingdom. The BBC exists by royal charter, its board of directors is appointed by the state, and it receives its funding from a government-enforced license fee on all television sets. Nonetheless, it retains complete editorial independence from the authorities. During the 80 years of its existence, the BBC has earned a worldwide reputation for the quality of its news and entertainment programming, and its radio World Service is listened to throughout the globe. The BBC's main competition comes from Independent Television (ITV), which was launched in 1955 to provide a commercially funded alternative. Unlike the BBC, which carries no advertisements, the ITV channels pay their way by selling advertising slots during program breaks. Both the BBC and ITV have come under pressure recently from satellite television companies such as Sky, which was established by Australian media tycoon Rupert Murdoch.

Murdoch is also the owner of several English newspapers, most famously the *Times*, which is one of the oldest and most influential papers in the world. Traditionally, England's newspapers were published in Fleet Street in London, but electronic printing techniques have allowed most papers to move beyond this cramped location to more spacious and modern sites. The

British press was traditionally divided into "broadsheet" and "tabloid" categories; the broadsheets, such as the *Telegraph* and the *Guardian,* were larger and more serious papers, while tabloids such as the *Sun* and the *Mirror* were often packed with lurid and sensational stories about celebrities, royalty, scandals, and gossip. In recent years, some of the serious newspapers such as the *Times* have abandoned their broadsheet format and adopted a tabloid one, claiming this was what their readers wanted. There are also a number of important political and literary magazines published in London, such as *The Economist,* the *New Statesman,* and the *Spectator.*

Movies are very popular in England, either rented for VCR or DVD players at home, or shown in public cinemas. Hollywood blockbusters tend to dominate the listings, though there is a small but quietly successful homegrown movie industry that produces high-quality films. England has produced many internationally famous film stars as we have already seen, but these have mostly tended to gravitate across the Atlantic to make their name in the United States rather than stay in the United Kingdom.

One highly significant aspect of modern life in England is the massive growth in "wired-ness" that has occurred in the last decade. In 2004, statistics showed that for the first time more than half of all households in England had a home computer. Of these, about 90 percent had online capability with connection to the Internet, and since 2006, there has been a huge increase in the provision of DSL (Broadband) connectivity. Quite apart from downloading music and the playing of computer games, this wired-ness has meant that a huge proportion of communications now use e-mail and, similarly, large amounts of shopping and the making of vacation and airline reservations is done online. England is among the leading nations in this respect and in recent years has shown that its people are eager to embrace every kind of technological advance from cell phones, to digital cameras, to computers, to whatever new developments come on the market.

TRADITIONS AND FESTIVALS

England has a rich folklore populated by many legendary heroes and villains, some of whom are fictional, but loosely based on real persons. As mentioned, Camelot's King Arthur and his Knights of the Round Table were most probably inspired by an authentic Romano-British monarch from the mid-fifth century A.D. who fought against the invading Anglo-Saxons, although his story obviously became much romanticized over time. Similarly, Robin Hood may have begun life as a Saxon bandit operating out of the wild northern forests of Sherwood in Nottinghamshire in defiance of King John's authority. Merry Men aside, however, it is extremely unlikely that he gave away much of his loot from the rich to the poor outside of ballads! A more recent example of a hero-outlaw is the eighteenth-century highwayman Dick Turpin, who was definitely a real historical figure caught and hanged for his many stagecoach robberies in 1739. According to popular tradition, Turpin was a chivalrous rogue of the Jesse James variety; in reality, however, he seems to have been a ruthless criminal who killed anyone who got in his way.

As a predominantly Christian country, England shares many of the same religiously based holidays and celebrations as the United States. English children eagerly await the arrival of Santa Claus like their American counterparts, although he is usually known there as "Father Christmas." Popular Yule-tide foods include roast turkey, steamed Christmas pudding, and mince pies. At the Christmas dinner table, all the guests pull "crackers" with one another. These are paper tubes with a black powder strip that sparks noisily when the cracker is ripped apart and which disgorge small novelties and printed jokes. The day after Christmas, December 26, is known in

England as Boxing Day. This derives from an old tradition of tradesmen going from door to door collecting their Christmas boxes, or gifts, from grateful customers. Nowadays, the custom has fallen out of fashion, but Boxing Day continues to be a national holiday on which post-Christmas sports matches are often scheduled.

One unique English celebration is Guy Fawkes' Night, or Bonfire Night, as it is sometimes known. It is held every November 5, although it is not a public holiday. This is the celebration of the foiling of a plot to murder the Protestant king James I and his Members of Parliament in 1605. Roman Catholic conspirators hired an assassin, Guy Fawkes, to hide barrels of gunpowder in the cellar under the House of Lords and detonate these during the formal opening of Parliament. Fortunately for the king and his nobles, the plot was uncovered and Guy Fawkes was publicly executed. This somewhat grisly spectacle is reenacted across the country every November, when children build bonfires and place an effigy, "the Guy," on the top. It is also the day when English people traditionally set off fireworks and sing:

> Remember, remember, the 5th of November,
> Gunpowder, Treason, and Plot!

One celebration connected with the British Royal Family is the magnificent ceremony at the Horse Guards Parade in London called "Trooping the Colour," when the queen inspects the flags (or "colours") of one of the British Army's footguard regiments. This marks the queen's official birthday and takes place on the first, second, or third Saturday in June. She also has a real birthday (April 21), although neither day is celebrated as a public holiday. More regularly, the queen's official London residence, Buckingham Palace, is host to a ceremony called the "Changing of the Guard," when the soldiers standing on sentry duty outside the palace are relieved from duty. These troops wear the ceremonial scarlet jackets of guardsmen and the large black bearskin caps called "busbies."

FOOD

English food has acquired a rather bad reputation over the years. Admittedly, some of the more bizarre names for dishes, such as toad-in-the-hole (sausages in batter), spotted dick (spongy steamed pudding), and bangers and mash (more sausages, this time with mashed potatoes) can sound a bit unappetizing. However, England boasts plenty of tasty original food. The traditional English breakfast of eggs, bacon, sausage, baked beans, fried mushrooms, and so on is a treat for the taste buds, although not perhaps the healthiest or most practical start to the morning.

Roast dinners of beef, chicken, or ham, with vegetables, potatoes, and Yorkshire puddings (pancake batter cooked in small pudding basins) as side dishes are equally popular later in the day. The English love to combine meats with pastries, creating such delicacies as sausage rolls (sausage meat in a flaky pastry) and pork pies. English cheeses, such as Cheddar, Stilton, Lancashire, and Wensleydale are justifiably world-renowned for their quality. Battered cod, plaice, or haddock and "chips" (fries) can be bought almost anywhere, and kippers (smoked herrings) are also popular fish. The influence of New Commonwealth immigration is certainly visible in the large number of Indian and Chinese restaurants that now proliferate England's towns and cities. These are very often more popular with the indigenous population than the restaurants that serve less exotic local English fare. But there is no mistaking that excellent food and a variety of different sorts of cuisine can be found throughout England in these times.

The English have two favorite beverages—beer and tea. English beer, known as "bitter," is traditionally drunk at room temperature and has a smooth, rich taste. Although the United Kingdom has mostly gone metric as regards weights and

Fish 'n' chips (battered fish and fries) is one of the most popular dishes in English cuisine. Restaurants and even small food stands like this one in the seaside town of Blackpool, in northwestern England, serve the meal.

measures in recent years, it is still considered sacred to serve beer in pints and half-pints in English pubs. The English love of afternoon tea is well known. Besides the beverage itself, no traditional afternoon tea would be complete without scones slathered with thick Devonshire cream and jam, as well as cucumber sandwiches, or cookies.

8

England's Heritage and Treasures

No book on England would be complete without some discussion of historical geography and the country's wealth of historic sites. Its rich and varied past has ensured that it is particularly blessed in this respect and, as we have mentioned, this is why England is a top destination for tourists from around the world. Although only a fraction of this heritage can be mentioned, let us consider some of the ancient sites and some of the finer castles, cathedrals, palaces, and great houses that merit the attention of scholars and tourists alike.

Some prehistoric sites in England date from Neolithic times and are unlike anything elsewhere in the world. Foremost of these is Stonehenge; and, also in Wiltshire, is Avebury, which comprises the largest stone circle in western Europe and an associated earthwork. Near Avebury is Silbury Hill, the largest prehistoric artificial mound in Europe, and West Kennet Long Barrow, a 350-foot-long chambered burial mound. These monuments are together recognized as a World Heritage Site by UNESCO. Other stone circles well worth visiting are to be found at Castlerigg in Cumbria, the Hurlers in Cornwall, and various ones in the Penwith district of West Cornwall.

There are many sites in Britain dating from the Roman era as we have seen, but the one that is most rewarding to visit is undoubtedly Bath. The Great Roman Bath itself and parts of the auxiliary buildings, together with the Temple of Sulis Minerva, have been excavated and put on display for visitors. The complex is mostly below the eighteenth-century Pump Room, which was built at a time when Bath again became a fashionable spa where people would take the waters. The whole city of Bath is designated a World Heritage Site, because in addition to its Roman remains, the extensive eighteenth-century Georgian architecture is unparalleled elsewhere in England. Other Roman sites of note include Housesteads Fort on Hadrian's Wall near Hexham in Northumberland, Fishbourne Roman Palace in West Sussex, and Lullingstone Roman Villa in Kent.

England boasts many medieval castles through its length and breadth, some ruined and some well preserved, and there are indeed many castles of more recent origin. Another World Heritage Site is the Tower of London, which has served as a fortress, a palace, and a prison since the time of its construction during the reigns of William the Conqueror and William II, his successor. Today, the tower houses England's national collection of medieval armor and arms, based on the arsenal of Henry VIII, and also the "Crown Jewels" belonging to the monarch and including elaborate gold crowns and other treasures.

Windsor Castle in Berkshire is the largest inhabited castle in the world, dating back to William the Conqueror, and has been continuously inhabited since the eleventh century. It is one of the principal residences that the British monarch Queen Elizabeth II uses to entertain guests on both state and private occasions. Massive outer walls enclose the castle's 11 acres, which contain many different buildings, including the great Round Tower, the State Apartments, the Queen's Private Apartments,

St. Michael's Mount in Cornwall is one of England's most spectacular castles. Built in the twelfth century, it is home to many attractions, including a terraced garden that includes a number of exotic plants.

and St. George's Chapel, where 10 British monarchs are buried. Rather than just a fortress, Windsor Castle is more like a self-contained small town, and it is one that today draws thousands of tourists from throughout the world.

Although there are many castles throughout England, some are spectacular by virtue of their dramatic setting. In this category, one would put St. Michael's Mount in Cornwall, which is built on a rocky island a quarter of a mile off the coast and accessible either by boat or by a causeway that is covered by the incoming tide twice a day. Originally a monastery and a center for pilgrimages, it was fortified and used as a fortress for much of its history, and so may be referred to as a castle. It now belongs to the National Trust, which conserves many historic British buildings and opens them to the public. Other notable, and indeed spectacular, castles in the care of the National Trust include Bodiam Castle in East Sussex, Sizergh Castle in Cumbria, the massive Castle Drogo in Devon (built as late as 1910–1930), and Sissinghurst Castle in Kent, which has one of the finest gardens in England.

Another part of England's architectural heritage is its cathedrals and its churches. In general, most of these historic ecclesiastical buildings belong to the Church of England and were built in the days before Henry VIII, when the Church was under Roman Catholic jurisdiction. Other religious denominations in the United Kingdom, including post-sixteenth-century Roman Catholics, had to acquire or build their own churches, because the Church of England did not willingly give up any of theirs until the last 50 years or so.

Canterbury Cathedral is the most famous and one of the oldest Christian buildings in England. Its first archbishop was St. Augustine of Canterbury who was sent from Rome in A.D. 597 to evangelize the English. He and his successors built the first Saxon church on this site. This was rebuilt and extended several times before being transformed in Norman times into the magnificent cathedral that we see today. Canterbury is the cathedral of the Anglican Archbishop of Canterbury, who is the Primate of All England—the religious leader of the Church. One archbishop, Thomas Becket, was murdered here on the steps of the High Altar in 1170. Yet again the king, at that time Henry II, was having trouble with the Church and its leader, the archbishop. His guards heard him say, "Who will rid me of this turbulent priest?" and two of them, taking it literally, rode to

Canterbury and slew the primate in his own cathedral. There is now a shrine to Becket, who became a martyr.

Another magnificent cathedral, which dates from 1093, is that at Durham in northeastern England. Its huge square towers rise high above the River Wear, and this historic building, together with Durham Castle, which faces it close by, has also been designated a World Heritage Site. It has been called "one of the great experiences of Europe to the eyes of those who appreciate architecture" by the writer on architecture Sir Nikolaus Pevsner, and more recently U.S. author Bill Bryson has written, "I unhesitatingly gave Durham my vote for best cathedral on planet Earth."

Lincoln Cathedral and Ely Cathedral in Cambridgeshire are also architectural masterpieces from much the same era. They both contain a wealth of Norman architecture, in particular Romanesque doorways with elaborately carved ornamentation, and much in the later Gothic style with high, pointed arches and clustered columns. Another gem is Wells Cathedral in Somerset, whose west front displays the most extensive array of medieval sculpture to survive in Britain. Inside this cathedral is a wonderfully elaborate mechanical clock dating from 1390 that has moving models of knights on horseback who fight a joust whenever the clock strikes.

Just five miles away is Glastonbury Abbey, or at least the ruins of a once mighty abbey that was even greater than Wells Cathedral. Glastonbury was the cradle of Christianity in England and, according to legend, Jesus's uncle St. Joseph of Arimathea used to travel there, on one occasion accompanied by his nephew. Some years after the Crucifixion, he is said to have returned with a band of followers and founded the first church in Britain at Glastonbury. Certainly this place soon became the greatest center of pilgrimage in England, and an abbey was founded there that became a most powerful monastic establishment. All this came to an end in 1539, when Henry VIII commanded the monasteries to be closed and disbanded. The abbot of Glastonbury was tried, convicted, and then hanged,

Part of Buckingham Palace, the Queen's Gallery is open to the public and houses items from the Royal Collection, including works from Renaissance artists Raphael and Titian. Here, a visitor examines Domenichino's *St. Agnes* and Tintoretto's *Esther before Ahasuerus* at the gallery.

drawn, and quartered on the nearby hill called Glastonbury Tor. Glastonbury also is central to the legend of King Arthur, and today there is still much of interest here connected with these mythical and mystical themes, making it something of a Mecca for those of a New Age persuasion.

Many of the ancient English cathedrals had palaces built beside them for the incumbent bishop. These are fine residences, some of which are open to the public, but they hardly compare with the magnificence of England's royal palaces such as Buckingham Palace, St James's, and Hampton Court. A palace is generally the official residence of a monarch, or a head of state, and is usually a large and lavish building as was thought to befit such an occupant. These days, some palaces, such as Hampton Court (which is no longer used by royalty), are open to the public, and even part of Buckingham Palace, the Queen's Gallery, is open to visitors. The latter is a treasure house of art that includes paintings by Dürer, Clouet, Rubens, Van Dyck, Claude, and Lely, works by Fabergé, as well as furniture, sculpture, and ceramics, jewelry, silver, and gold. As we have noted, the Palace of Westminster is the formal name for the U.K. parliament, but use of the word *palace* here merely reflects its earlier role as a royal residence.

Almost the only great palace in England that was never a royal residence is Blenheim Palace in Oxfordshire. This was built from 1705–1722 for the duke of Marlborough as an extraordinary honor when the house was given to him by a grateful nation in recognition of his successful role as army commander in the War of the Spanish Succession against the French between 1701 and 1710. Vast and opulent, this palace is both a treasure house and a national monument. Its fame and attraction has also been increased by the fact that Britain's more recent wartime leader, Sir Winston Churchill, was a member of this family and was born in Blenheim Palace in 1874.

Besides palaces and castles, England has a wealth of historic and stately homes such as Wilton House, Chatsworth, Burghley House, Houghton Hall, and Longleat to name but a few. All of these and many others are accessible to paying visitors.

England's heritage is the embodiment of its history and of its changing fortunes. To understand the role that England has played in Western civilization, the reader who has not already been there should definitely consider visiting its shores.

CHAPTER

9

England Looks Ahead

In 1962, U.S. Secretary of State Dean Acheson famously remarked that: "Great Britain has lost an Empire, and not yet found a role." By this he meant that the United Kingdom was still basking in its old imperial glory. All of its colonies were fast disappearing, and the country was finding it difficult to adjust to the new reality of being an ordinary, middle-sized European state. In the same way, it might be possible to say that England in the twenty-first century is slowly losing its smaller empire—the United Kingdom—without yet finding an alternative role. This is not a completely new development. As noted, one large part of the British Isles, Southern Ireland, left the United Kingdom in 1922. However, the increasing desire of the other parts of the United Kingdom—Scotland, Wales, and Northern Ireland—for greater political autonomy has put the long-term future of the United Kingdom in its present form in some doubt.

Preserving the traditions of the monarchy is an important aspect of English culture. Pictured here is the queen's procession during the 2002 Golden Jubilee, which marked the fiftieth anniversary of Queen Elizabeth II's ascension to the throne.

It is certainly too early to write off the United Kingdom as a nation-state. Although the Scots, Welsh, and Northern Irish have made it clear that they would like a greater say in the day-to-day workings of their own regions, there is as yet no majority in any one of them for complete independence. A BBC poll taken in Scotland in early 2007, for instance, showed that only 32 percent of Scotland's population favored complete independence from the rest of the United Kingdom when answering the question, "Would you like the Union [with England] to come to an end?" The figures for other parts of the United Kingdom are currently less than this. Membership in the United Kingdom has economic and political benefits, as well as costs, and there is plenty of residual loyalty toward the old institutions of the state, especially the Royal Family. Many men and women who remember the fight for Britain during the twentieth century's two world wars remain fiercely proud that they are citizens of the United Kingdom. Regional parliaments may actually have pacified the demand for complete independence. It will be interesting to see whether the pro-separatist political parties in the "Celtic fringe," as the non-English parts of the United Kingdom are sometimes called, continue to make headway in the new century.

Whether Britain survives or not as a concept, it seems clear that regional identities within the United Kingdom are becoming more important. Where does this leave England? As the people at the heart of the British state, the English have to some extent diluted their own national consciousness in favor of a larger British identity. For example, the English patron saint, the dragon-slayer St. George, has his saint's day on April 23 every year. But there is no public holiday, or organized celebrations of this day, in the same way that there are for St. Andrew in Scotland on November 30, St. David in Wales on March 1, or St. Patrick in (both parts of) Ireland on March 17. Many English people are not even aware of the correct date of St. George's Day. Another example is the national anthem that is played at international soccer matches; the Scottish, Welsh, and Northern Irish teams have special anthems of their own, but the England squad uses the general British anthem "God Save the Queen." In the past, English soccer fans waved the Union Jack at their games, rather than the more technically correct Cross of St. George (the horizontal and vertical red cross on a white background at the center of the Union Jack), although they certainly use this latter flag now. Small details such as this demonstrate how Britain and England have become synonymous in people's minds, including the minds of many English themselves.

Symbols aside, there is also the more practical question of England and the rest of the United Kingdom's relationship with the United States and Europe. For decades, presidents and prime ministers have spoken of the special relationship between the United States and the United Kingdom based on ties of language, custom, and wartime and peacetime alliances. On the other hand, Britain is increasingly connected to events taking place in the European Union, which, with its recent creation of a single currency, seems to be moving inexorably toward greater federal union. These competing relationships leave the United Kingdom's future path unclear. Imperial Britain's old ability to remain friendly but aloof from both continents is now next to impossible. It remains to be seen whether the country can juggle its North American and European interests at the same time without having to commit to one or the other.

Today, England is one of the world's most powerful nations, as it has been for hundreds of years. This is despite the fact that the twentieth century was a period of almost constant decline of England's international power and prestige and, with the survival of the British political union looking rather less certain at least in its present form, one might be tempted to guess that the twenty-first century will also be a grim epoch for England. But that is taking much too pessimistic a view. England's role may change, but whatever happens, it will remain an important country with a unique and precious culture all its own. During World War II, there was a popular sentimental song called "There'll Always Be an England." It has been true for at least a thousand years now, and will no doubt remain true long into the future.

Facts at a Glance

Note: All figures refer to England specifically unless listed as (U.K.), which means that they are figures for the United Kingdom as a whole.

Physical Geography

Location Western Europe, southern portion of the island of Great Britain in the British Isles, in the Atlantic Ocean off the northwestern European mainland between the North Atlantic Ocean and the North Sea

Area Total: About 50,000 square miles (130,000 square kilometers), roughly the area of Alabama

Boundaries *Border countries:* Scotland, 108 miles (174 kilometers); Wales, 133 miles (214 kilometers)

Coastlines 3,415 miles (5,496 kilometers)

Climate Temperate; moderated by prevailing southwest winds over the North Atlantic Current; more than one-half of the days are overcast

Terrain Mostly rugged hills and low mountains in the north; level to rolling plains in east and southeast

Elevation Extremes Lowest point is The Fens, −13 feet (−4 meters) below sea level; highest point is Scafell Pike, 3,210 feet (978 meters)

Land Use Arable land, 2.85%; permanent crops, 0.38%; other, 96.77% (2006)

Irrigated Land 4,614 square miles (11,950 square kilometers) (2005)

Natural Hazards Winter windstorms; floods

Natural Resources Coal, petroleum, natural gas, tin, limestone

Environmental Issues Deforestation; pollution of rivers and coastal waters from municipal sewage and industrial/agricultural/mining runoff and wastes

People

Population 50 million [U.K., 60,776,238 million] (July 2006 est.); males, 30,077,548 (2006 est.); females, 30,698,690 (2006 est.)

Population Density 930 per square mile (360 per square kilometer)

Population Growth Rate 0.28% (England has dropped below the replacement level fertility rate of 2.1 percent; growth is the result of immigration)

Net Migration Rate	2.17 migrant(s)/1,000 population (U.K., 2007 est.)
Fertility Rate	1.66 children born/woman (U.K., 2007 est.)
Birthrate	10.67 births per 1,000 population (U.K., 2007 est.)
Death Rate	10.09 deaths per 1,000 population (U.K., 2007 est.)
Life Expectancy at Birth	Total population: 78.5 years; male, 76 years; female, 81 years (U.K., 2006 est.)
Median Age	total: 39.6; male, 38.5; female, 40.7 (U.K., 2007 est.)
Ethnic Groups	White, 93%, black 2%, Indian 1.8%, Pakistani 1.3%, mixed 1.2%, other 1.6 (2001 census)
Religion	Christian (Anglican, Roman Catholic, Presbyterian, Methodist), 71.6%; Muslim 2.7%; Hindu 1%; other 1.6%; unspecified or none 23.1% (U.K., 2001 census)
Language	English
Literacy	(Age 15 and over can read and write) Total population: 99% (99%, male; 99%, female) (2003)

Economy

Currency	Pound sterling
GDP Purchasing Power Parity (PPP)	$ 1.903 trillion (U.K., 2006 est.)
GDP Per Capita	$31,400 (U.K., 2006 est.)
Labor Force	31.1 million (U.K., 2006 est.)
Unemployment	2.9% of total population (U.K., 2006 est.)
Labor Force by Occupation	Services, 80.4%; industry, 18.2%; agriculture, 1.4% (U.K., 2006 est.)
Agricultural Products	Cereals, potatoes, vegetables, cattle, sheep, poultry
Industries	Machinery and transportation equipment, electrical goods, food products, chemicals, textiles
Exports	$469 billion (U.K., 2006 est.)
Imports	$603 billion (U.K., 2006 est.)
Leading Trade Partners	Exports: U.S., 13.9%; Germany, 10.9%; France, 10.4%; Ireland, 7.1%; Netherlands, 6.3%; Belgium, 5.2%; Spain, 4.5% (U.K., 2006 est.). Imports: Germany, 12.8%; U.S., 8.9%; France, 6.9%; Netherlands, 6.6%; China, 5.3%; Norway, 4.9%; Belgium, 4.5%; Italy, 4% (U.K., 2006 est.)
Export Commodities	Manufactured goods, fuels, chemicals, food, beverages, tobacco
Import Commodities	Manufactured goods, machinery, fuels, foodstuffs

Transportation	Roadways: 241,097 miles (388,008 kilometers), all of which are paved (2004), including 2,187 miles (3,520 kilometers) of expressway; Railways: 10,660 miles (17,156 kilometers); Airports: 471–334 are paved runways (2006); Waterways: 1,988 miles (3,200 kilometers) (U.K., 2006 est.)

Government

Country Name	England (part of the United Kingdom of Great Britain and Northern Ireland)
Capital City	London
Type of Government	Constitutional Monarchy, with two legislative houses (elected House of Commons and nominated/hereditary House of Lords)
Head of Government	Prime Minister Gordon Brown (since June 2007)
Independence	England has existed as a unified entity since the tenth century
Administrative Divisions	47 boroughs, 36 counties, 29 London boroughs, 12 cities and boroughs, 10 districts, 12 cities, 3 royal boroughs

Communications

TV Stations	288 (U.K., 1995 est.)
Radio Stations	650 (AM, 219; FM, 431)
Phones	94,034,000 (including 61,091,000 cell phones)
Internet Users	37.6 million (U.K., 2005 est.)

* Source: *CIA-The World Factbook* (2007)

500000 B.C.	Suggested date for first evidence of Paleolithic inhabitation of Britain.
6000	Rising sea levels cut off Great Britain from the European mainland.
4000	First evidence of agriculture (Windmill Hill civilization).
2000	First evidence of bronze-working (Beaker People); Stonehenge believed to have been constructed between 2500 B.C. and 2000 B.C.
700–300	Celtic civilization arrives in England; first evidence of ironworking.
55	Julius Caesar's Roman troops raid southern England.
A.D. 43	Roman emperor Claudius orders permanent occupation of England ("Britannia").
60	Queen Boudicca unsuccessfully revolts against Roman invaders.
410	Roman settlers in England are informed that they can no longer rely on Rome's imperial protection against incursions by barbarian invaders.
Fifth Century	Waves of pagan Anglo-Saxon tribes invade England; original Romano-British inhabitants flee or assimilate; England subdivided into kingdoms (Wessex, Mercia, Northumbria).
Seventh Century	Anglo-Saxons converted to Christianity.
Ninth–Tenth Centuries	Vikings raid, and then occupy, Northumbria.
927	Athelstan of Wessex reunites England as a single kingdom.
1066	William of Normandy claims English throne after the death of St. Edward the Confessor; his invading army kills King Harold at the Battle of Hastings.
1086	Normans compile the *Domesday Book* recording English land, tax, and population details.
1215	Magna Carta, a statement of limitations of the rights of the English king, is signed by King John under duress from the barons.
Thirteenth Century	Monarch begins to call parliaments to discuss laws and tax increases.
1283	Wales united with England.
1337–1453	Hundred Years' War between England and France; ends with loss of most of English royal lands in France.

1455–1485	War of the Roses between the houses of York and Lancaster; ends with the death of the Yorkist Richard III at Battle of Bosworth Field and ascent of Henry VII of the House of Tudor.
1533	Henry VIII breaks with Rome and founds the Church of England.
1539	Dissolution of the monasteries.
1558–1603	Reign of Elizabeth I, seen as a golden age of literature and exploration; also the rise of English naval power; Spanish Armada unsuccessfully attempts invasion of England (1588).
1603	James I (James VI of Scotland) succeeds to the English throne and becomes first king of Great Britain.
1607	First successful English settlement in North America (Jamestown, Virginia).
1641–1645	Civil War between forces of Charles I and Parliament; ends with Charles's defeat and execution (1649); England becomes a republic under Oliver Cromwell (1649–1660).
1660	Restoration of the monarchy under King Charles II.
1688	"Glorious Revolution" overthrows Catholic James II and invites Dutch Protestant William of Orange to take over the throne.
1707	Act of Union between England and Scotland combines the parliaments and creates the United Kingdom.
1750–1850	Main years of Industrial Revolution (approximately).
1783	Great Britain makes peace with new United States of America.
1801	Ireland, occupied by England intermittently since the twelfth century, officially joins United Kingdom.
1837–1901	Reign of Queen Victoria; sees a large expansion of the British Empire across South and East Asia and in Africa; the "Pax Britannica" during which Great Britain is acknowledged as the dominant world power.
1914–1918	First World War; the United Kingdom emerges victorious over Germany but with grievous human and financial losses.
1939–1945	Second World War; the United Kingdom again victorious against Germany and its allies but with still greater monetary losses; Winston Churchill prime minister.

1945–1951	Labour Party government creates Welfare State system; India becomes independent (1947) and British Empire slowly begins to unravel.
1952	Queen Elizabeth II becomes monarch.
1979–1990	Margaret Thatcher's Conservative government reforms many aspects of the British economy.
1997	Tony Blair becomes Labour Prime Minister.
2005	Fifty-two people killed in London Underground by suicide bombers.
2007	Tony Blair resigns and Gordon Brown becomes the new prime minister.

Bibliography

Coones, Paul, and John Patten. *Penguin Guide to the Landscape of England and Wales.* New York: Penguin, 1986.

Gardener, Juliet, and Neil Wenborn, eds., *The Columbia Companion to British History.* New York: Columbia University Press, 1996.

Heath, Anthony, and Clive Payne. *Twentieth Century Trend in Social Mobility in Britain.* Oxford, UK: CREST: Centre for Research into Elections and Social Trends, 1999.

Lee, Phil, and Rob Humphries. *The Rough Guide to England.* London: Rough Guides, seventh edition, 2006.

Oakland, John. *British Civilization,* sixth edition. New York: Routledge, 2006.

The Official Yearbook of the United Kingdom (HMSO, 2005). Available online at *http://www.statistics.gov.uk/StatBase/Product.asp?vlnk=5703*

Paxman, Jeremy. *The English: A Portrait of a People.* New York: Overlook, 2001.

Toth, Susan Allen. *England for All Seasons.* New York: Ballantine, 1998.

White, Robert. *A Short History of England.* Cambridge, U.K.: Cambridge University Press, 1967.

Statistics from *Encyclopedia Britannica,* the *CIA World Factbook,* and the 2006 *New York Times Almanac.*

Wikipedia—The Free Online Encyclopedia. Available online at *http://en.wikipedia.org/wiki/Main_Page*

Books

Baker, Alan R. H., and Mark Billinge, eds. *Geographies of England: The North-South Divide, Imagined and Material.* New York: Cambridge University Press, 2004.

Hibbert, Christopher. *The Story of England.* London: Phaidon Press, 1994.

Tompson, Richard S. *Great Britain: A Reference Guide from the Renaissance to the Present.* New York: Facts on File, 2003.

Web sites

English Culture
http://www.britainexpress.com/History/english-culture.htm

CIA World Factbook—United Kingdom
https://www.cia.gov/cia/publications/factbook/geos/uk.html

Geography of England
http://www.k12academics.com/england_geography.htm

A Vision of Britain through Time
http://www.visionofbritain.org.uk/index.jsp

Index

actors and actresses, 59
agriculture, 78–80
airports, 84
American War of Independence, 38
Anglican Church. *See* Church
    of England
Anglo-Saxon invasions, 32
antisocial behavior, 55–56
architectural heritage, 104–109
Arthur, King, 21, 99, 108
artists, 59
Athelstan, 33
automobile usage, 84
Avon River, 22

Bath, 104
Battle of Britain, 41
BBC (British Broadcasting
    Corporation), 97
Beaker people, 29–30
Becket, Thomas, 106–107
beer, 101–102
Birmingham, 22
Black Death, 34
Blair, Tony, 67–68
Blenheim Palace, 109
BNP (British National Party), 47
bombings of London
    Underground, 48
Bonfire Night, 100
boroughs, 70
Boudicca, 31
Boxing day, 100
Bristol, 22
Britain. *See* Great Britain
Britannia, 30, 32
British Broadcasting Corporation
    (BBC), 97
British Commonwealth, 42. *See also*
    Commonwealth of Nations
British English, 51, 52
British Isles, 9–11, 14–16
British National Party (BNP), 47
broadcasting, 97
Brown, Gordon, 68

bubonic plague, 34
Buckingham Palace, 63, 100–101, 109

Canterbury Cathedral, 106–107
castles, 104–106
cathedrals and churches, 106–108
Catholic Church, 53
cattle industry, 79–80
Celts, 30, 31
Changing of the Guard, 100–101
Channel Tunnel, 13, 14, 16, 85–86
Charles I, 37
Charles II, 37
Christian religions, 31, 32, 52–54
Christmas holiday, 99–100
Church of England, 34, 36, 52–53
churches, 31, 106–108
Churchill, Winston, 41, 109
civil war of 1640s, 37
class structure, 54–56
Clean Air Act (1956), 25
climate, 17–18
coal, 76–77
coastline, 16–17, 26
colonial empire, 40–41, 42
Common Market. *See* European
    Union
Commonwealth of Nations, 13, 63. *See*
    also British Commonwealth
computer use, 98
Conservative Party (Tories), 69
constitution, 61–62, 73–74
Cornwall, 21
counties (shires), 70–71
Crick, Francis, 59
cricket, 95
crime, 89
Cromwell, Oliver, 37
cuisine, 101–102
Cumbria, 24, 25
currency, 87–88

Dark Ages, 32–33
Darwin, Charles, 58
dialects, 51–52, 55

Dickens, Charles, 59
Disraeli, Benjamin, 80
Domesday Book, 33
Durham Cathedral and Castle, 107

East Anglia, 22–23
economy
    agriculture, 78–80
    European Union and, 86–88
    fishing industry, 80
    Industrial Revolution and, 39–40
    manufacturing and heavy industry,
        80–81
    natural resources, 76–78
    overview, 75–76
    service sector, 81–84
    trade, 86
    transportation, 84–86
education system, 92–95
Edward III, 33–34
Edward VI, 36
Edward VIII, 62
EEC (European Economic Community).
        See European Union
elections, 66
Elizabeth I, 36
Elizabeth II, 62–63, 100
Ely Cathedral, 107
Empire period, 40–41, 42
energy production, 77–78
England
    domination of British Isles by, 11
    as part of Great Britain, 9
    as part of United Kingdom, 11
English Channel, 14
English language, 50–52, 55
entertainment, 97–98
environmental concerns, 25–26
euro, 87–88
European Economic Community
        (EEC). *See* European Union
European Union (EU), 76, 86–88, 113
Eurotunnel (Channel Tunnel), 13, 14,
        16, 85–86
exports, 86

family life, 89
Faraday, Michael, 58
farming, 78–80
festivals, 99–100
feudal system, 33
fishing industry, 80
flag, 9, 112
flooding, 26
food, 101–102
foot-and-mouth disease, 79–80
foreign influences, 27–28, 44
France, Plantagenet claim to throne of,
        33–34
French Revolution, 38–39
future challenges, 110–113

GDP (Gross Domestic Product), 75
geography
    British Isles, 9–11, 14–16
    climate, 16–17
    land features, 16–17
    Midlands and East Anglia, 22–23
    Northern England, 23–25
    Southern England, 19–22
    Yorkshire and Northwest England, 23
George VI, 62
Glastonbury Abbey, 107–108
Glorious Revolution, 37, 64
government and politics
    the monarchy, 62–63
    overview, 61–62
    Parliament, 63–66, 73–74
    political parties, 66–70
    reforms of, 73–74, 110–112
    regional government, 70–71
Great Britain, 9, 11, 14–15
Greater London, 21, 71
Gross Domestic Product (GDP), 75
Gulf Stream, 17–18
Guy Fawkes' Night, 100

Hadrian's Wall, 31
health care system, 91–92
Henry II, 106–107
Henry VII, 34

Index

Henry VIII, 34–36, 107
highways, 84
historic sites
    cathedrals and churches, 106–108
    medieval castles, 104–106
    palaces, 108–109
    prehistoric, 103–104
    Roman era, 104
history
    American War of Independence, 38
    birth of Britain, 36–37
    British civil wars and revolutions,
      37–38
    Dark Ages, 32–33
    Empire period, 40–41, 42
    foreign influences and, 27–28, 44
    French Revolution, impact of, 38–39
    Industrial Revolution, 39–40, 45
    Norman conquest and Middle Ages,
      33–34
    post–World War I developments,
      41–42
    prehistoric period, 28–30
    Roman occupation, 30–31
    War of the Roses and Reformation,
      34–36
holidays, 99–100
House of Commons, 65, 73–74
House of Lords, 65–66
housing, 91
human habitation, earliest, 28, 44
Hundred Years' War, 34

immigration, 13, 44, 45, 47–49
imports, 86
independence movement, 110–112
Independent Television (ITV), 97
Industrial Revolution, 39–40, 45
industry, heavy, 22, 80–81
international influence, 11–12, 110, 113
Internet use, 98
invasions, 27, 44
Iraq, 68
Ireland, 9, 37
Irish Rebellion, 41

Irish Sea, 16
ITV (Independent Television), 97

James I, 36
James II, 37
Jewish population, 54
Julius Caesar, 30

kings. See specific names, e.g., James I

Labour Party, 67–68, 90
Lancashire, 23
language, 50–52, 55
legendary characters, 99
leisure activities, 96–97
Liberal Democratic Party, 69–70
Lincoln Cathedral, 107
livestock industry, 79–80
Livingstone, Ken, 71
Lloyds of London, 82–83
London
    as economic center, 13
    as financial center, 82–83
    fog/smog of, 25
    geography, 21
    government of, 71
    as tourism attraction, 83
    transportation in, 84
London Stock Exchange, 82–83
London Underground bombings, 48

mad cow disease, 79–80
Magna Carta, 63
Major, John, 69
manufacturing, 80–81
maps, 10, 15
Mary I (Bloody Mary), 36
media, 97–98
Members of Parliament (MPs), 65
Middle Ages, 33–34
Midlands, 22–23
mining, 77
monarchy, 62–63, 73
motorways, 84
movies, 98

MPs (Members of Parliament), 65
Murdoch, Rupert, 97
music business, 83–84
musicians, 60
Muslim extremists, 48, 54
Muslim population, 54

Napoleon Bonaparte, 38–39
Napoleonic Wars, 38
national anthems, 112
National Health Service (NHS), 91–92
National Union of Mineworkers
    (NUM), 77
natural resources, 17, 76–78
New Commonwealth British, 13,
    47–49
newspapers, 97–98
Newton, Isaac, 56–58
NHS (National Health Service), 91–92
nonwhite immigrants, 47–49
Norman Conquest, 33–34
Norsemen, 32–33
North Sea, 16, 77
Northern England, 23–25
Northern Ireland, 11, 110–112
Northumberland, 24, 25
Northwest England, 23
nuclear reactors, 77–78
NUM (National Union of
    Mineworkers), 77

Opticks (Newton), 58
Orwell, George, 43, 44, 55

palaces, 108–109
parishes, 70
Parliament, 63–66, 73–74
Pax Britannica, 40–41
Peers of the Realm, 66
Pennines, 23
people
    influential persons, 56–60
    New Commonwealth British, 13,
        47–49
    population trends, 44–47

settlement and early immigration,
    44–45
    uniqueness of, 43–44
*Philosophiae Naturalis Principia
    Mathematica* (Newton), 57
Plantagenet kings, 33–34
political parties, 66–70
politics. *See* government and politics
pollution, 25–26
population trends, 44–47
precipitation, 18
prehistoric period, 28–30
prehistoric sites, 103–104
prime minister, 65
private schools, 94–95
Protectorate, 37
public schools, 94–95

queen, role of, 62. *See also* specific
    names. For example, Victoria

race relations, 47–49
railroads, 84–85
rainfall, 18
Reformation, 34–36
regional government, 70–71
religion, 31, 32, 52–54
Republic of Ireland, 9
Richard III, 34
Robin Hood, 99
Rolling Stones, 83–84
Roman Catholic Church, 53
Roman historic sites, 104
Roman occupation, 30–31
rugby, 95

saints' days, 112
Scafell Pike, 25
schools, 92–95
scientists, 56–59
Scotland, 9, 11, 14, 36, 110–112
separatist movement, 110–112
service sector, 81–84
Shakespeare, William, 8–9, 22, 56
shipping, 86

Index

shires (counties), 70–71
Six Counties, 11
Smith, William, 17
soccer, 95
social structure, 54–56
social trends, 89–90
Southern England, 19–22
Spanish Armada, 36
sports, 95–96
St. Michael's Mount, 106
stone circles, 29–30, 103–104
Stonehenge, 29–30, 103

tea, 102
television broadcasting, 97
terrorist attacks, 48, 54
Thames River, 20–21
Thatcher, Margaret, 69, 90, 91
Tories (Conservative Party), 69
tourism, 83
Tower of London, 103
trade, 86
traditions and festivals, 99–101
Trafalgar, Battle of, 38, 40
trains, 84–85
transportation, 84–86
Trouping the Colour, 100
Turpin, Dick, 99

U.K. See United Kingdom
Ulster, 11
United Kingdom (U.K.). *See also*
    England; Scotland; Wales

birth of, 36–37
constituent countries of, 11
future of, 110–112
Gross Domestic Product of, 75
international relationships of, 113
regional identities and, 112–113
United States, relationship with, 113
universities, 93–94
urbanization, 45

Victoria, 40
Vikings, 32–33

Wales, 9, 11, 14, 36, 110–112
War of the Roses, 34
Washington, George, 60
Watson, Charles, 59
weather conditions, 17–18
Welfare State system, 90–92
Wells Cathedral, 107
Wessex, 32, 33
Westminster Palace, 65
William of Orange, 37, 64–65
William the Conqueror, 33
Windmill Hill, 28–29
Windsor Castle, 104–105
women, role of, 90
World War I, 41
World War II, 41–42
writers, 59

Yorkshire, 23

page:

About the Contributors

ALAN ALLPORT was born in Whiston, England, and grew up in East Yorkshire. He has an M.A. in history from the University of Pennsylvania and is currently a Ph.D. candidate there, with a special interest in nineteenth- and twentieth-century European history. He is the author of *American Military Policy, Freedom of Speech,* and *Immigration Policy* in Chelsea House's POINT/COUNTERPOINT series.

GEORGE WINGFIELD is a graduate of Trinity College in Dublin, Ireland, where he earned both a B.A. and an M.A. in natural sciences. Wingfield has worked as an astronomer at the Royal Greenwich Observatory and as an engineer and consultant for IBM. He has contributed to a number of books on the crop circle phenomenon in Britain and, in 1992, presented a lecture on the topic at the Smithsonian Institution and appeared on the *Larry King Show.* He currently leads tours of ancient and sacred sites in England, Scotland, and Ireland.

CHARLES F. GRITZNER is distinguished professor of geography at South Dakota State University. He is now in his fifth decade of college teaching and research. Much of his career work has focused on geographic education. Gritzner has served as both president and executive director of the National Council for Geographic Education and has received their George J. Miller Award for Distinguished Service.